Intelligent Guide

Napa Valley

2021 edition

Benjamin Lewin MW

Copyright © 2020, 2021 Benjamin Lewin

ISBN 9781674219363

Vendange Press

www.vendangepress.com

Preface

This guide covers Napa Valley, or perhaps I should say Napa Valleys, since it covers not only the valley proper, running from Napa to Calistoga, but also the various mountain areas on either side that are part of the general Napa AVA. Carneros is included in the Guide to Sonoma.

The first part of the guide discusses the region, and explains the character and range of the wines. The second part profiles the producers. There are detailed profiles of the leading producers, showing how each winemaker interprets the local character, and mini-profiles of other important estates.

In the first part, I address the nature of the wines made today and ask how this has changed, how it's driven by tradition or competition, and how styles may evolve in the future. I show how the wines are related to the terroir and to the types of grape varieties that are grown, and I explain the classification system. For each region, I suggest reference wines that illustrate the character and variety of the area.

In the second part, there's no single definition for what constitutes a top producer. Leading producers range from those who are so prominent as to represent the common public face of an appellation to those who demonstrate an unexpected potential on a tiny scale. The producers profiled in the guide represent the best of both tradition and innovation in wine in the region. In each profile, I have tried to give a sense of the producer's aims for his wines, of the personality and philosophy behind them—to meet the person who makes the wine, as it were, as much as to review the wines themselves.

Each profile shows a sample label, a picture of the winery, and details of production, followed by a description of the producer and winemaker. Each producer is rated (from one to three stars). For each producer I suggest reference wines that are a good starting point for understanding the style. Most of the producers welcome visits, although some require appointments: details are in the profiles. Profiles are organized geographically, and each group of profiles is preceded by maps showing the locations of producers to help plan itineraries.

The guide is based on many visits to Napa and other regions of the North Coast over recent years. I owe an enormous debt to the many producers who cooperated in this venture by engaging in discussion and opening innumerable bottles for tasting. This guide would not have been possible without them.

Benjamin Lewin

Contents

Tables

Appellation Maps

Producer Maps

The Importance of Napa

When the famous Napa Valley Welcome signs were erected in 1949 at each end of the valley, the concept of Napa as a world-famous wine growing region was no more than wishful thinking. Production had scarcely recovered from Prohibition, there were more prune trees than grapevines, and the grape varieties were mostly low quality for bulk production, with less than 5% Cabernet Sauvignon. The original sign carried the names of the members of the Napa Valley Vintners Association who erected it: there were only nine of them.

Napa Valley did not became a serious wine-producing area until the 1960s, but by the 1970s it was the standard bearer for the New World's challenge to Europe. Until the famous Judgment of Paris tasting in 1976, when Cabernet Sauvignon and Chardonnay from Napa Valley placed ahead of Bordeaux and Burgundy, there was little interest in wines from outside Europe. The tasting changed the situation dramatically; Napa Valley, and in due course other places in the New World, were taken seriously, starting the trend to consider wines in terms of single grape varieties. Yet at the time, there were few inklings in Napa that their wines were about to play a major part on the world stage.

The news of the tasting came as a shock in Napa. The immediate effect was to sell out the wines that had won—the Chateau Montelena Chardonnay and Stags Leap Cabernet. But the more important, longer term effect was to validate the concept of high-end wines from Napa. Bo Barrett of Chateau Montelena recollects that up to then, it had been an uphill battle to get the wines into distribution on the East Coast. "The practical consequence was that distributors would take the wines," he says. The effect on style was to reinforce the view that Napa should compete with Bordeaux. "The Paris tasting had the effect that if we won there, we must be as good, and we should make wine more like Bordeaux," says Fred Schrader.

An irony is that the Chateau Montelena Chardonnay did not really come from Napa. The grapes were sourced 50% from Sonoma County's Alexander Valley, 40% from Russian River Valley, and only 10% from Napa Valley. This in itself demonstrates the great change over fifty years from then regarding winemaking as paramount to now regarding sources as all-important.

After the Judgment of Paris, Napa began to focus on Cabernet Sauvignon. At the start of the twentieth century, wine labeled as "Claret" was more than half of production, but it rarely contained any of the Bordeaux varieties. Prohibition abolished any thoughts of moving to quality, and when it was

Napa Valley is a monoculture of vines all the way across the valley floor.

repealed, Alicante, and Carignan were two-thirds of plantings in California. White varieties had disappeared. The trend towards mass production varieties continued for the next half century. A huge proportion of wine was sold as an alternative to spirits at the very low end, and became known as the "Skid Row Trade."

When the move to quality started in the 1970s, bulk production varieties still accounted for more than 80% of all production. In whites, Colombard (not a variety usually associated with quality) was the major variety with 40% of plantings. Today, Bordeaux varieties account for 80% of black plantings, and Chardonnay accounts for almost 70% of white plantings.

Some date the modern era in Napa from 1966, when Robert Mondavi opened his winery, the first new winery to be built in Napa since Prohibition. New wineries have been the driving force in Napa's revival: three quarters of Napa's current 400 wineries have been established since 1966, and it's a striking measure of change that you can count on the fingers of one hand the number of producers profiled in this guide who even existed in 1970. Initially vineyards replaced prune orchards on the valley floor, and then the move began to clearing virgin land to plant mountains on the hillsides.

Napa Valley likes to present an artisanal impression. "95% of the wineries are family-owned," says the Napa Valley Vintners Association. This is somewhat misleading as half of the vineyard land is distributed among several hundred owners, but the other half is owned by fewer than 25 individuals or

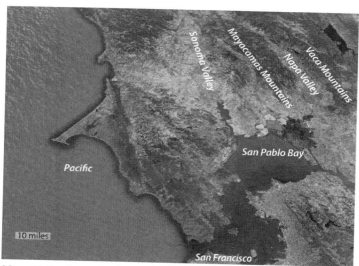

Napa Valley is north of San Pablo Bay, and about an hour from San Francisco.

corporations. The largest owners have hundreds of acres; the smallest has only a couple. The ten largest owners (headed by conglomerate Treasury Wine Estates) hold almost one third of the vineyards, The median vineyard holding is about 85 acres.

The increasing price of land pushes a trend towards concentration as the owners of the first wave of expansion from the 1970s-1980s come up to retirement: some estates pass to the next generation, but others sell to a large corporation. This is balanced by the creation of new wineries by enthusiasts, but the rising price of land, and increasing restrictions on winery construction, with limits on how much wine can be produced and how many visitors are allowed each day, makes this more difficult. The high cost of entry now requires significant resources, leaving the artisan vintner squeezed between conglomerates and lifestyle wineries. For small estates, custom crush wineries sometimes offer an easier option than constructing a winery. The surprising fact is that, in spite of high prices for their wines, only a minority of Napa Valley wineries are actually profitable.

Varietals versus Blends

Today Napa Valley is closely associated with Cabernet Sauvignon, but Cabernet Sauvignon production was insignificant until the 1970s. Asked whether Cabernet Sauvignon was the obvious variety of choice when Joseph Phelps was established in 1973, Bill Phelps says, "Hardly. The first three years Riesling was the main variety. It wasn't clear Cabernet would be the future until the late seventies. At the start we planted Riesling, Pinot Noir, and Cabernet Sauvignon. During the 1980s we realized we couldn't do every variety and we focused on Cabernet Sauvignon."

As it became clear that Cabernet Sauvignon should be the black grape of choice, what were the producers' stylistic aims? When you decided on Cabernet, were you trying to compete with Bordeaux, I asked Bill Phelps? "Absolutely. The model was the first vintage of Insignia in 1974. Joe made it like a Bordeaux and really wanted it to be a blend." Have objectives changed since the first vintage? "Our style has changed. This was a decision. As Napa came into its own, we realized what was in the material and we could rely on the vineyards. In the 1970s, things were driven by winemaking, now they are more driven by what happens in the vineyards. There's still a strong affinity with Bordeaux, but now we have established our own identity."

Once Cabernet Sauvignon was established as the principal grape, if it was blended with other varieties in Napa, they were the usual suspects: Merlot, Cabernet Franc, and Petit Verdot. A split developed between those who believe that pure Cabernet Sauvignon gives the best results and those who believe that blending produces more complex wines, and this continues to the present.

Wines labeled as Cabernet Sauvignon are allowed to include 15% of other varieties in most New World countries, and up to 25% in the United States. A large proportion of wines labeled as Cabernet Sauvignon in Napa in fact are just over the 75% limit, so it would be a fine line to distinguish them from blends dominated by Cabernet Sauvignon.

Varietal-labeled Cabernet Sauvignon is Napa's main challenge to Bordeaux. The main alternative consists of Bordeaux blends with less than three quarters Cabernet Sauvignon, and most often these are described as Proprietary Reds. A category called Meritage, introduced in 1988 to describe wines based on a Bordeaux blend, never really impacted the mainstream, and has mostly disappeared.

Chardonnay has taken over as Napa's main white representative, and Sauvignon Blanc has become firmly established in second place. Both tend to show rich styles, especially for Sauvignon Blanc when it is vinified in the Fumé Blanc style pioneered by Robert Mondavi, using barrel fermentation in oak (sometimes new oak, at that). Both Chardonnay and Sauvignon Blanc are usually vinified to make single varietal wines.

Fog in Napa Valley

Napa Valley itself is quite a confined area. About 30 miles long and generally less than a mile wide, it nestles between the Mayacamas mountains to the west (separating Napa from Sonoma) and the Vaca mountains to the east. Looking across the valley, a difference is immediately apparent between the Mayacamas Mountains, which are covered in vegetation, and the Vaca Mountains, which have a distinctly scrubby appearance. Weather comes from the Pacific, and the east is drier than the west, because rainfall gets blocked by the Mayacamas Mountains.

Napa Valley has an abundance of that surprising key feature for wine production in California: fog. This is not usually welcome in wine-producing regions, but the climate in California would normally be too warm for fine wine production, and is rescued only by the regularity of the cooling fog. Almost all the top regions for wine production are in valleys that are cooled by fog rolling in from the Pacific Ocean. (The exceptions are vineyards at high enough elevations that cooling comes from the altitude.) Morning fog is fairly reliable in Napa, usually clearing around midday.

Fog rolls into Napa Valley from the Pacific most mornings, and disperses around midday.

The Mayacamas Mountains to the west are covered in evergreens.

Because a high pressure system settles over the California coast each summer, the growing season tends to be warm and dry. Except for the absence of rain in the summer, the climate is perfect for agriculture. Irrigation fills the gap. Although most vineyards in Napa are irrigated, there is a slowly growing movement towards dry farming (meaning no irrigation). According to Christian Moueix, when he came from Petrus to establish Dominus: "I was determined to have dry farming (apart from the very young vines)... Dry farming encourages deep roots and is key for expressing terroir. I have not had the success I had hoped for to convince my friends to give up irrigation, they say the vines will die. No, they come from the Caucasus and can withstand anything. Unirrigated vines will naturally find their equilibrium and won't need to be picked as late as irrigated vines. Irrigation is one of the reasons you get these crazy alcohol levels in Napa."

The climate in Napa Valley escapes the European rule that temperatures become warmer going south; the northern end is decidedly warmer than the southern end, because the more open southern end gets cooling breezes from San Pablo bay, whereas the narrow northern end is effectively closed. At the very southern end, Napa itself is close in temperature to Bordeaux; but Calistoga at the far north is more like the south of France, and it becomes too hot to grow Cabernet Sauvignon on the valley floor.

The hot, dry nature of the climate was brought home forcefully with the wildfires that raged in northern California in 2017, and 2019. Few vineyards in Napa or Sonoma were directly damaged, but there were issues with possible smoke taint, as it's very difficult to remove from grapes that have been exposed. Producers who harvested before the fires were less at risk. In 2017

The hills to the east are dry and scrubby.

and 2019 most of the damage occurred after harvest, but then in 2020, as well as destroying around 30 wineries, the fires created smoke taint made it impossible to use grapes that were still on the vine, and a majority of grapes were not even harvested.

The damage in 2020 was worst at the northern end of the valley. Fires started in August, and then the major Glass Fire started east of St. Helena near the Silverado Trail on September 27 and burned well into October. "From south St. Helena to north of Calistoga, the hillside is completely charred," Frank Dotzler at Outpost Wines said. "A drive through the valley now, it's just unimaginable." There was extensive damage on Spring Mountain, Diamond Mountain. and Howell Mountain.

Climate and Terroir

Definition of individual regions, or more specifically identification of those locations where particular varieties grow best, developed slowly after the growth of the 1960s. The spur for the realization that not all sites in Napa Valley were created equal was the definition by University of California professors Albert Winkler and Maynard Amerine in the 1940s of heat zones in Napa Valley. Classifying California into five zones according to average temperatures during the growing season, they recommended suitable grape varieties for each region. Among the varieties recommended for the cooler, southern part of Napa Valley were Cabernet Sauvignon and Chardonnay, but it was not until the 1960s that growers paid much attention.

Wildfires came close to vineyards in Napa and Sonoma at the end of the seasons from 2017 to 2020..

With the extension of grape growing from the valley floor (where it resumed after Prohibition) to the mountain slopes (planted after the revival of the seventies), there is considerable variation not only of terroir but also of climate. In fact, the most important determinant of climate may be elevation, rather than position along the valley. The original definition of heat zones mapped Napa into three zones, with the Carneros region at the southern end the coolest in zone 1, Napa itself in zone 2, but Oakville and St. Helena in warmer zone 3. More recent data confirm a gradual increase in average growing season temperatures going up the valley, but put the whole valley floor into zone 4 (making it marginal for Cabernet Sauvignon), with conditions becoming significantly cooler moving up in elevation into the mountains on either side.

To the casual tourist—of whom there are more than five million annually—driving up Route 29 on the western side, or back down the Silverado trail on the eastern side, Napa Valley might appear quite homogeneous, a veritable sea of vines stretching across the valley between the mountains on either side. The land appears flat until close to the mountains. Taking any cross street between the two highways, you travel exclusively through vineyards. The Napa river in the center of the valley seems unimportant. The impression of dense plantation is true for the center of the valley, where three quarters of the land is planted with vines, but this apparent consistency is somewhat deceptive.

The collision between the three tectonic plates that created the valley some 150 million years ago left detritus of a great variety of soil types, with more than 40 different soil series classified in Napa. A major factor is the consistent difference between the warmer, and more fertile, valley floor, and

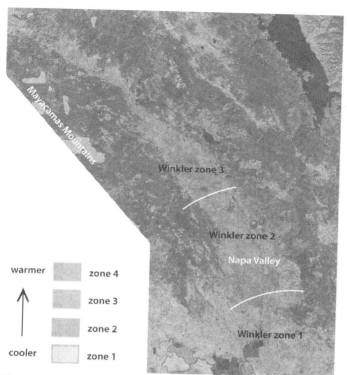

Climate mapping by Winkler originally divided the valley into three zones, becoming increasingly warmer going from south to north. More recent data suggest the main difference is between the valley floor and the slopes and mountains on either side.

the cooler terrain of the slopes to the west and the east. And moving from south to north, the soil changes from sediments deposited by past oceans to a more volcanic terrain, which also is prevalent on the mountains.

The heart of the valley is characterized by alluvial fans, formed by streams that flowed out of the mountains. When a stream opens out on to a valley floor, it deposits sediment as it flows. Over time, the sediment causes the watercourse to shift sideways, creating a fan-like area of sediment, stretching from the slopes to the valley floor. Alluvial fans run continuously along the west side of the valley; the series is more broken up along the east side. Known locally as "benches," the most famous are the Oakville Bench and the Rutherford Bench, where production of fine wine started in the nineteenth century.

Valley floor tends to be used in two senses in Napa. Generally used as generic description to distinguish terrain between the mountain ranges as

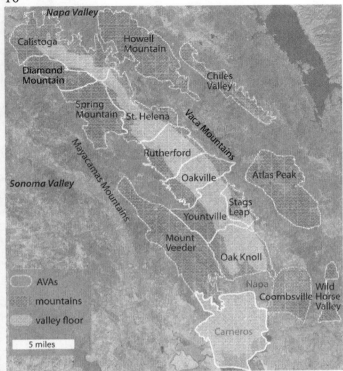

Napa AVA has many smaller AVAs within it. AVAs on the west and eastern sides are mountainous, but those in the center extend across both slopes and valley floor. (Carneros connects Napa and Sonoma valleys.)

opposed to the steep slopes, it is not pejorative. Sometimes it is used more disparagingly to distinguish fertile soils from the alluvial fans. Sediments become finer, and the soils that form on them become richer, as an alluvial fan widens out. Beyond the fan, soils on a valley floor can be too rich for producing fine wine.

"Terroir isn't everywhere. In fact, terroir is in very few places. I have five wines and one is a terroir wine," says Doug Shafer of Shafer Vineyards. "Hillside Select is a special place; it's planted with one hundred percent Cabernet Sauvignon, but it could be Merlot or Cabernet Franc and the special quality of the fruit would still come through." Doug feels that hillsides make better wine than flat lands, but that the gap has narrowed. "Originally we didn't have the tools to make wines from the valley floor. Changes in viticulture mean now you can make wine from the valley floor that is nearly as good as the hillside. You have to work harder; we used denser planting and canopy management to reduce yields. This was not possible ten years ago."

Napa and its AVAs

Well before any regulations were introduced, Napa Valley became an imprimatur of quality on the label. Following the precedent of the French system of appellation contrôlée, the AVA (American Viticultural Area) system was introduced in 1976. This defines a pyramid of wine-producing regions. A broad Napa Valley AVA covers the whole region: as the result of a highly political process, the boundaries go well beyond the valley itself and were drawn to include all vineyards regarding themselves as producing Napa Valley grapes. Covering a total area of 90,000 ha, which represents about half of Napa County, the AVA has about 18,500 ha of vineyards. Given the variation between the south and north, and between the valley floor and the mountains, this implies a certain lack of coherence.

AVAs are defined at the instigation of producers in a region, and there are presently fifteen smaller AVAs within the all-encompassing Napa Valley designation. They extend from appellations defining the central valley to mountainous slopes on either side. (Producers often use the term appellation rather than AVA, and will talk about their appellation or sub-appellation wines.) The sub-AVAs tend to have more integrity, and often indicate higher quality wines. About 40% of the vineyards are in the old areas, stretching from Yountville through St. Helena, at the heart of the valley. Almost all the Napa AVA is covered by a sub-AVA, except for a few areas east of the valley.

Are there really discernible differences between AVAs in the valley? The answer is yes and no. There may be a core to each sub-AVA, but unfortunately the same sorts of political considerations came into play when

Bryant Vineyards is the Pritchard Hill area at an elevation of 130m overlooking Lake Hennessey. It is within the St. Helena AVA.

Napa Valley AVAs in Capsule

Calistoga is the far north and narrowest point of the valley. Chateau Montelena has a historic reputation, Eisele Vineyard has special terroir.

St. Helena extends around the town of St. Helena but stretches to the slopes of Spring Mountain to the west and to Pritchard Hill at the east. Vineyards run all the way from Spring Mountain to the west to Pritchard Hill to the east.

Rutherford is the heart of the valley with the top vineyards on the Rutherford Bench, making wines that are among the most elegant from the valley proper. Inglenook is the famous old name.

Oakville shares the core of the valley with Rutherford, but is perhaps a little more powerful. Robert Mondavi is in the valley, Harlan is off to the west, and Screaming Eagle is on the Silverado Trail.

Stags Leap is one of the smaller AVAs with vineyards clustered around the Silverado Trail and is known for the velvety, lush quality of its tannins. Shafer Vineyards is the standard bearer today.

Yountville has never established any great reputation in its own name, but has the classic character of the valley proper. Dominus is its most famous vineyard.

Oak Knoll is just a touch cooler than the appellations in the heart of the valley.

Coombsville is a relatively new AVA for the area south of the town of Napa, and is the coolest area in the valley; producers are focusing on Chardonnay.

defining the sub-AVAs that had much reduced the coherence of Napa AVA. The original proposal for Stags Leap District, for example, expanded to the west, south, and north as producers on the edges clamored to be let in.

The boundaries of the AVAs don't always make it easy to tell whether a particular wine has come from a valley or mountain. The AVAs in the valley often extend up the slopes of the mountains on either side. Pritchard Hill is well known for mountain Cabernets from the vineyards of Bryant, Chappellet, and Colgin, at elevations ranging from 120-330m—but is included as part of the St. Helena AVA, together with vineyards on the valley floor.

Unlike the European system, the statement of an AVA on the label applies only to geographical origin; there is no additional implication of quality, grape variety, or style. When the rules were being discussed in 1979, André Tchelistcheff was sarcastic about the construction of AVAs. "We are not solving the basic elements of appellation, we are not controlling the varietals, we are not controlling the maximum production; I mean we are just trying to fool the consumer that we have appellation of origin."

An AVA label only requires that 85% of the grapes come from the AVA: my view is that this is nowhere near good enough. Considering the premium you pay for Napa Valley, a wine labeled from Napa should have only grapes from Napa. As for vintage, the rules have finally been tightened to specify that wine from an AVA must have 95% of its grapes from the stated vintage. For grape variety, the rule is 75%; this is probably as good as we are going to get, since it started out as 51% when the first federal regulations were introduced in 1936, and was increased (against some opposition) to 75% in 1983. The 75% rule leaves a lot of wiggle room, far too much in my opinion. I would like to see all the rules replaced with a 95% lower limit!

The Rutherford-Oakville Bench

The most famous appellations of the valley proper have the most distinct reputations. The supposed characteristic of Rutherford is a dusty note in the wines. Whether Rutherford Dust is real or is a marketing ploy has long been debated. "The tannins of wines from Rutherford give the sensation you get by running your hand backwards along velvet," was an imaginative description by one producer.

I do find a similar quality to the tannins in the wines of several producers. I would not describe it as dusty, more as a sort of distinctive tannic grip. But there are other producers whose wines typically have more massive or tighter

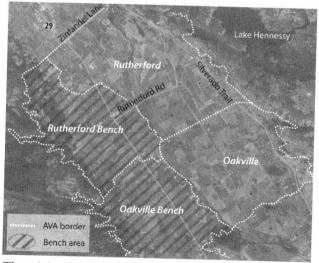

The original proposal for AVAs in 1989 included separate AVAs to distinguish between the benches to the west and the areas of Rutherford and Oakville on the valley floor. The height limit for the AVAs on both sides of the valley was 500 ft. The proposal was not approved. While it's difficult to define the exact region of the benches, as a rough working rule, vineyards to the west of route 29 show more of the supposed character of the AVA than those to the east.

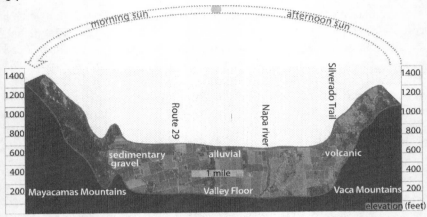

A cross section of the valley through the Oakville AVA shows variety of soil types and exposures to the sun.

tannins. I would be prepared to concede a commonality in which firm tannins give the wines a quality I might be inclined to call Rutherford Grip, but more to the point, I find the wines of Rutherford always to have a slight aromatic lift that I do not find elsewhere.

Oakville shows a character of taut black fruits supported by fine-grained tannins that reinforce an impression of elegance. "Oakville is about expressing big berry fruits, a rich character with black olives, and more open tannins," says Mark de Vere of Mondavi. Some wines display a much softer style, with more overt, opulent black fruit aromatics extending from blackcurrants to cassis, and you might argue that they have deserted the communal specificity by going for more approachability in their vinification, but otherwise it is fair to say that Oakville is usually more powerful than Rutherford.

The problem with the AVAs in the heart of valley—Oakville, Rutherford, St. Helena—is that their reputation has been defined by the vineyards on the western side, running towards the slopes of the Mayacamas Mountains (basically by the classic region of the Oakville-Rutherford bench). While these may have consistent characters, the case for coherence is undercut by the extension of the AVAs right across the valley (and sometimes beyond it).

Soils change from sedimentary gravel at the west to alluvial in the valley floor and to volcanic at the east. Exposure changes from the cooler morning sun of the western side to the hotter afternoon sun of the eastern side. What is valid along route 29 may very well not apply to the Silverado Trail.

The heart of Napa Valley, between Napa and St. Helena, has a monoculture of vineyards, extending across the narrow valley, confined by the mountains on either side.

Stags Leap

"Cabernets in Stags Leap tend to have richer fruit, with a softer texture," says Doug Shafer, who was instrumental in establishing the AVA. Shafer's Hillside Select, one of the top wines of the AVA, which comes from the vineyard rising up behind the winery, epitomizes this quality, with a style of opulent fruits showing evident aromatics. Doug supports his case by recollecting that when Shafer showed its first 100% Cabernet Sauvignon, it was so approachable that people refused to believe it had no Merlot.

Stags Leap is one of the smaller AVAs, with more coherence in its terroir than most, confined to the eastern side of the valley just under the Silverado Trail. But in Stags Leap District today, I get less impression of consistency, with many wines that are forward and approachable, showing soft black fruits on the palate, supported by nuts and vanillin on the finish, and tannins noticeable only as a soft, furry presence in the background. These are nice enough for something to drink immediately, but I wonder how it represents Cabernet typicity to make wines that are so fruit-forward and lacking in tannic structure. Again it's a producer's choice, but it seems more common in Stags Leap.

There may be a typicity that distinguishes each AVA if you let it express itself. In any of these appellations, however, you can make soft, forward, fruity, wines with lots of nutty vanillin, using appropriate winemaking techniques to bump up the appeal. Let's at least say that unless you know the producers' styles, the name of the AVA has little predictive value.

Famous Vineyards in the Valley

In Europe, wines made from grapes grown on the estate are often regarded as having higher quality than wines made from purchased grapes. The situation is a bit different in Napa and Sonoma, where there is a healthy market in grapes, and some of the most expensive grapes have come from vineyards where growers are famous for the quality, but sell the grapes rather than bottling themselves. Growers have been a driving force for quality in Carneros and Sonoma; the effect is less marked in Napa, but there are still cases where the name of the vineyard is as important as the name of the producer, although they are becoming fewer as the vineyards are sold and become monopoles of individual producers. It is surprising how many of the famous vineyards were first planted in the nineteenth century.

Some of the top sites in Napa Valley have long histories, with potential that was recognized more than a century ago. At the heart of the Oakville area is the To Kalon vineyard, a parcel of almost 100 ha originally purchased by Hamilton Crabb in 1868 (the name is Greek for "most beautiful"). Further purchases brought Crabb's total to more than 150 ha. Half of the land was planted with hundreds of grape varieties within a few years. Wine was produced under the name of To Kalon vineyards; the best known was "Crabb's Black Burgundy," which actually was made from the Italian Refosco grape. But Cabernet Sauvignon was also grown there in the 1880s.

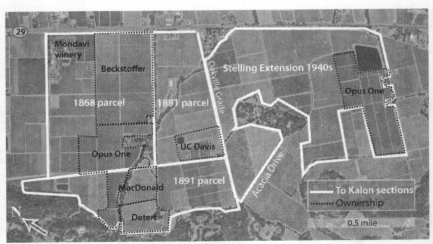

The original 403 acre To Kalon vineyard was assembled by Hamilton Crabb between 1868 and 1891. Martin Stelling extended it by 275 acres in the 1940s. Robert Mondavi (now Constellation) is the major owner (all parts not marked as another owner). Opus One and Beckstoffer own large parcels and there are three other small parcels.

Looking down the To Kalon vineyard from the apex of the alluvial fan, there's a slight gradient down to route 29. The scrubby hills beyond the Silverado trail are in the background.

After various vicissitudes, including changes of ownership, Prohibition, and destruction of the original winery, the vineyard fell into various hands. In the 1940s, Martin Stelling bought the original vineyard and a large plot of similar size adjacent to it, and called it all To Kalon. The major part eventually ended up with Robert Mondavi, whose new winery was positioned at the edge of the original To Kalon vineyard. Mondavi trademarked the name To Kalon, and can in fact use for grapes from anywhere; producers buying grapes from other parts can use the name only for wines from those grapes.

A minor (89 ha) part of the original To Kalon estate was purchased by Beaulieu Vineyards in 1940, and became the heart of Beaulieu's Private Reserve, but was sold to Andy Beckstoffer in 1993. Beckstoffer sells grapes to a variety of producers, and some of Napa Valley's most expensive Cabernets come from this parcel. It's a measure of the reputation of the vineyard that grapes from the best-known parts sell for close to ten times the average price for Napa Valley Cabernet Sauvignon.

The last, smallest part of the original To Kalon vineyard is a parcel of 8 ha that Crabb himself donated to the University of California; this now forms their Oakville Experimental Station. (Probably the most expensive terroir for an experimental station anywhere in the world!)

The To Kalon vineyard occupies the top half of the Oakville Bench—the apex of the fan is more or less at the top of the vineyard. The terroir is a gravelly loam, forming a gradual slope (only just noticeable to the eye) from an elevation of about 75m at the base of the mountains to 50m at the highway. Its expansion has made To Kalon is very large for a high quality vineyard, so

The eucalyptus trees at the edge of Martha's Vineyard may have something to do with its famous minty aroma. The Opus One block of To Kalon is on the far side of the trees.

it has significant variation. "Up by the hills it's grand cru terroir, and the wine goes into the Reserve, towards the middle it's premier cru level, and the wine goes into the Oakville Cabernet, down by route 29 it's village territory and the wine goes into a Napa bottling," says Mark de Vere at Mondavi.

Just above the To Kalon vineyard is Heitz's famous Martha's Vineyard. The Martha's Vineyard 1974 was the first wine from Napa that fooled me at a blind tasting into thinking it came from Bordeaux. I had to be shown the bottle to be convinced I had made a mistake. This hundred percent Cabernet Sauvignon comes from a 35 acre vineyard on the Oakville Bench, just above the To Kalon vineyard. The vineyard itself is not easy to find; there are no signs or directions—perhaps Heitz don't want it covered in day trippers.

The vineyard was owned by Tom and Martha May, and after a handshake deal, Joe Heitz started to produce wine from its crop in 1966. It was one of the first single vineyard wines of the modern era. The wine is often said to have a minty taste, and even the Heitz web site mentions the string of eucalyptus trees at the edge of the vineyards close to the base of the mountains, but Joe Heitz is reputed to have believed that the mintiness actually was a property of the vines (which are claimed to come from a proprietary clone producing unusually small berries). (But when Opus One acquired a block of the To Kalon vineyard on the other side of the trees, they did not like the minty taste in their wine, and cut down some of the trees.)

With some shade from the mountains close by, Martha's Vineyard is a little less sunny than some others; possibly this contributes to a slightly cooler climate impression and lower alcohol. "For more than two decades, Heitz Martha's Vineyard was the benchmark by which California Cabernets were judged," said Frank Prial of the New York Times in 2000. More recently it has of course followed the inevitable trend towards greater extraction and higher alcohol, but the wine remains relatively restrained for Napa. 1974 probably remains its greatest vintage.

Just across the road from Mondavi, Opus One was one of the first collaborations between Bordeaux and Napa. When Robert Mondavi and Baron Philippe de Rothschild announced the venture, it was seen as a validation of Napa as a winemaking region. Opus One is a Bordeaux blend dominated by Cabernet Sauvignon (around 85%). An even clearer example of French influence on Napa is Dominus winery, located on the old Napanook vineyard, one of the first vineyards in Napa Valley, planted on the Oakville alluvial fan by George Yount in 1838. The vineyard was bought in 1943 by John Daniel, owner of Inglenook, and he kept it when he sold Inglenook in 1970.

Dominus was first produced as a partnership between Christian Moueix of Petrus in Pomerol and John Daniel's daughter, and then in 1995 Christian became sole owner. The change in varietal constitution over the years is one sign of the adjustment from Bordeaux to Napa. "When Dominus started we had 21% Merlot; now it's only 0.2%. Cabernet Sauvignon has gone from 65% to 85%. The initial plantings were prejudged from Bordeaux, that you could transpose percentages from Bordeaux to Napa and it would work," says winemaker Tod Mostero.

Some Historic Vineyards					
Vineyard	Location	Owner	# producers	First Planted	Acres
Dr. Crane	Saint Helena	Beckstoffer	10	1858	25
Hayne	Saint Helena	Hayne	4	1900s	13
Haynes	Coombsville	Gaylord Lawrence	7	1960s	32
Tofanelli	Calistoga	Tofanelli	4	1920s	20
Martha's Vineyard	Rutherford	May Family (Heitz)	1	1963	40
To-Kalon	Oakville	6 owners	34	1872	678
Stagecoach	Atlas Mountain	Gallo	90	1992	600

Stagecoach Vineyard takes its name from a site where a bandit in the nineteenth century robbed the stagecoach in the pass between St. Helena and Monticello. It was planted with vines at the end of the century, and the grapes fetched record prices. It was abandoned by the time of Prohibition, and not planted again until Dr. Jan Krupp and his brother bought the 1,300 acres on Pritchard Hill in Atlas Mountain AVA in 1995. It took 7 years to clear the land, and $4 million to plant vines. Today the 600 acre vineyard is one of the most famous in Napa. It has a red volcanic soil on a rocky base. Stagecoach supplied grapes for high-priced bottlings by more than 90 producers, and it was a shock when it was sold to Gallo in 2017 for $180 million. As existing contracts for grape purchases expire, those releases may cease to exist. (Krupp Brothers retained some blocks, from which they produce wine.)

Mountain AVAs

The area of the Napa Valley AVA extends far beyond the obvious tourist trails. Well off to the east are Howell Mountain, Chiles Valley, and Atlas Peak. To the west are Diamond Mountain, Spring Mountain, and Mount Veeder. Driving up the twists and turns of the densely forested roads into the mountains is a completely different experience from meandering along the center of the valley. Mountain vineyards are sparsely planted, occupying perhaps 5% of the total land, contrasted with the monoculture in the valley itself.

The big difference in Napa is really between mountains and valley: these have different climates and soils. With vineyards often above the fog line, the climate in the mountains is quite distinct from the valley itself, where fog is the dominant (and saving) influence. The playoff is that temperatures are reduced by the elevation, but increased by the lack of fog. There is often more diurnal variation. Mountain vineyards have primary soils with more mineral or volcanic character, compared with the more alluvial soils deposited by water flow in the valley. Couple the climatic changes with the differences in the soils, and you may well ask what connection exists between the mountain vineyards and those in the valley to justify labeling under the same AVA.

There's a growing tendency to plant Cabernet Sauvignon on hillsides and mountains rather than on the valley floor, and today about 14% of the vineyards and 20% of the wineries are on the mountains (mountain vineyards tend to be smaller). There is quite a bit of talk in Napa about "mountain tannins." Grapes grown on the mountains tend to have higher, and sometimes more aggressive, tannins; getting the tannins ripe at higher altitudes may require a long hang time, with the incidental consequence of later harvests. The grapes protect themselves from the combination of more sunshine (es-

Vineyards in the mountains have significant elevation above those in the valley itself, and conditions are quite different.

Napa Mountain AVAs in Capsule

Diamond Mountain was one of the first mountain areas to be planted, notably by Diamond Creek, which has stayed true to its character since the beginning. The formal name is Diamond Mountain District, because most of the mountain is actually over the border into Sonoma County.

Spring Mountain (formally Spring Mountain District) has vineyards all the way across from Napa to Sonoma County, with the Pride winery at the summit making cuvees from plots on both sides. The style is not as taut as Diamond Mountain.

Mount Veeder was an early mountain region, characterized by Mayacamas Vineyards. Wines tend to be classically restrained.

Howell Mountain is restricted to vineyards above the fog line. Soils are low in fertility, vines can be stressed, wines can be taut. Dunn Vineyards is the epitome of the old style.

Chiles Valley is obscure and very few wines are labeled with the AVA.

Atlas Peak is rugged territory, with vineyards along the two roads running on either side of the mountain. Tannins can be aggressive. Kongsgaard is its most famous winery.

Wild Horse Valley is really off the beaten track, well away from Napa Valley, and relatively obscure.

pecially higher ultraviolet radiation) and greater wind exposure by increasing their production of anthocyanins and tannins. All this contributes to a tighter structure, especially when the vineyards are above the fog line.

The mountains are not all the same. On opposite sides of the valley, Mount Veeder and Howell Mountain give the most taut impression of a fine backbone to the fruits. Atlas Mountain tannins are quite fierce: you have to go to the greater fruit intensity of the single vineyard wines to balance them out. Spring Mountain tannins are less obvious, not so much aggressive as just flattening the fruits.

When Hamilton Crabb planted the To Kalon vineyard, it was just a matter of clearing the land and digging in the grapevines. Switching the use of the land to viticulture, especially as it becomes a monoculture, creates a certain change in the environment, but the terroir remains recognizably the same. This has not necessarily remained true as vineyard plantings have extended to mountains. When the first vineyards were carved out of mountain sites around Napa in the 1960s and 1970s, no one thought much of it (aside from questioning whether the sites were appropriate for the intended varieties).

By the 1980s, people began to object to terraforming. One trigger was the construction of Atlas Peak Vineyards. As described by the project manager, Dick Peterson, "There are D10 Cats up there. This is a moonscape, but we're ripping it. We'll put terraces in there...We'll fill that canyon with rocks the size of Volkswagens, then cover it up with some muck from the caves we're digging."

Mountain reconstructions became controversial. When Delia Viader constructed her vineyard on Howell Mountain, environmental damage to Bell Canyon Reservoir below led to civil law suits and criminal charges. Today the growth of mountain vineyards has slowed dramatically. Given the much higher costs associated with creating and maintaining mountain vineyards, it's not surprising that they should include a concentration of high-end wineries; indeed, many of Napa's cult wines come from mountain sites.

Perhaps at the end of the day (environmental issues aside) the question is not whether a terroir is natural or artificial, but whether it is good for growing grapes. Or in the context of Cabernet Sauvignon, what's the difference in making wine from grapes grown on a mountain as opposed to in the valley? Indeed, it's a different approach for Napa to focus on mountain vineyards for growing Cabernet Sauvignon. Bordeaux is pretty flat, and the principal distinction between sites there is whether they are gravel-based or clay-based. Christian Moueix thinks there is a problem. "In Napa the current obsession is with elevation and hillside sites. I think hillside vineyards are a big mistake. They need irrigation and anyway it's not a natural habitat for vines."

Bill Harlan at Harlan Estate (on the mountain above Oakville) and Al Brounstein at Diamond Creek Vineyards (on Diamond Mountain) were pio-

Viader Vineyards is on Howell Mountain (although outside the AVA) on a 32-degree slope overlooking Bell Canyon (a source of the drinking water supply for St. Helena).

neers in believing that vineyards in the valley would not give the small berries that they needed for the highest quality Cabernet Sauvignon. "I wanted to create a first growth in California. All at once I started looking for a totally different type of land that would produce the best fruit, not necessarily look nice. Historically the best wine produced in America over a long period of time was the Rutherford Bench, but after studying soils I became convinced we wanted to be on the hillside with good drainage," says Bill Harlan. "Al felt that grapes from hillsides suffer more, and would give more intensity," Phil Ross at Diamond Creek recalls.

The Move to Ripeness

Napa's view on the appropriate style for Cabernet Sauvignon has evolved. As Napa began its revival, the general view was that Bordeaux was about elegance, and California was about power. Initially Napa Valley set out to compete with Bordeaux, but by the 1990s came around to the view that the wine should be in a richer style more reflecting its warmer climate. This has been the basis of a continuing debate as to whether Cabernet Sauvignon (and for that matter wines based on other varieties) should reflect the character of the places where they originated in Europe, or should show a more "international" style reflecting the new places where they are made.

Harlan Estate, which made one of the first "cult" wines in Napa, is on the mountain slopes at Oakville, looking out over Martha's Vineyard, To Kalon, and Napanook, lower in the valley.

Fred Schrader, who has been associated with cult wines since the early nineties, thinks the change in style is an appropriate reflection of conditions in Napa. "In the mid eighties, people wanted to make wine just like Bordeaux. I was never part of that school, my attitude was why do we care? The climate and actually the seasons here are different. We have a hotter climate, with riper berries; we are more fruit forward. We should not try to emulate, we should try to make something that reflects who we are."

The style changed in the early nineties. "When I was running Beaulieu, by the late eighties, we were trying to change the style of our wines," says Anthony Bell. "By the mid nineties we were in our stride. Probably the period from 1990-1995 was when things changed." Anthony quotes a telling example of the change in style. "Today the reserve wines are made from grapes picked at the end of the season, but when I joined BV the Reserve was made from grapes picked first—because they came from the healthy vineyards that gave the best quality grapes."

The move to the riper, more "international" style was partly driven by critics who scored the wines highly—or perhaps more to the point, scored restrained wines poorly. Many people feel that influential critic Robert Parker had a major effect in driving the trend, especially the singling out of "100 point" wines that were almost always powerful and fruit-driven.

Attempts at a European aesthetic in Napa were criticized. There was a long-running difference of opinion between Mondavi and the *Wine Spectator* over style. The *Spectator's* lead critic on California, James Laube, commented in July 2001, "At a time when California's best winemakers are aiming for ripe, richer, more expressive wines, Mondavi appears headed in the opposite direction... [Winemaker] Tim Mondavi and I have different taste preferences... He has never concealed his distaste for big, ultra rich plush or tannic red wines. I know he can make rich, compelling wines, yet he prefers structured wines with elegance and finesse... the attempt to give his wines more nerve and backbone has come at the expense of body and texture... he's decided to turn his back on a climate ideally suited for producing ripe, dramatic wines, and rein in those qualities so that the wines show restraint rather than opulence."

Tim Mondavi replied, "I am concerned... that while global wine quality has improved tremendously, there appears to be a current trend toward aggressively over-ripe, high in alcohol, over-oaked wines that are designed to stand out at a huge tasting rather than fulfill the more appropriate purpose of enhancing a meal."

There you have the whole debate in a nutshell. It's hard to defy the rush to ripeness: the price is likely to be lack of critical acclaim. Over recent decades, the story of Cabernet Sauvignon in Napa has been the struggle to control its ripeness. The same is true of other varieties: over-ripeness is the main reason why Merlot has not been successful and why producers have backed away from Chardonnay.

A Lack of Old Vines

Napa's character as a young wine region was prolonged by the need to replant many of the vineyards in the nineties. One of the glories of old vineyards is the extra concentration produced in the wine as the vines age. There's no exact measure for what the French would call Vieilles Vignes, but after about twenty years, the yields drop. Perhaps because the lower yields are achieved naturally, the extra concentration seems to have a focus and intensity that is not produced by simply reducing yields by extreme pruning. You might expect the vineyards that were planted during the boom of the 1970s now to have venerable old vines. Unfortunately, a problem with phylloxera put paid to that.

Because of its European origins, Vitis vinifera has no resistance to phylloxera; it must be grafted on to resistant rootstocks from American species of Vitis. Early plantings in Napa used the St. George rootstock, a cultivar of Vitis riparia, which is highly resistant to phylloxera. Its disadvantage is that it can lead the vine to be too productive. New plantings during the 1960s and 1970s

Because the focus on Cabernet Sauvignon is recent, there are not many old vines in Napa Valley. These fifty-year-old vines in the Kronos vineyard are among the oldest.

tended to use AxR1, a rootstock recommended by the Enology Department at the University of California, Davis for its reliability. AxR1 is a hybrid between Vitis vinifera and Vitis rupestris; like many hybrids with some vinifera parentage, it is not really very resistant to phylloxera. The university should have known better, because by the late 1980s, quite predictably, phylloxera was enthusiastically feeding on these rootstocks; unfortunately, by then about 75% of plantings in Napa and Sonoma were on AxR1.

The need to replant vineyards in the 1990s was not entirely a bad thing. "As growers were forced to replant by phylloxera, a lot of the unspoken issues—rootstocks, clones, spacing—became issues for discussion," says Anthony Bell, who had been horrified to find when he came to Beaulieu in 1979 from South Africa that Napa had made itself so vulnerable by planting on a single rootstock. "This was something all Europeans had been told you didn't do," he says.

Any vines more than, say, 60-years-old are likely to be Zinfandel. The only old Cabernet vines in Napa today are those planted on St. George before the phylloxera epidemic. Sometimes this was the result of calculation, sometimes it was luck, and sometimes *force majeure*. When Al Brounstein created Diamond Creek Vineyards in 1968, he was under pressure to plant AxR1, but he stuck to St George because it had a good record in the mountains. When Cathy Corison purchased her vineyard in Rutherford in the 1990s, the price was reduced because it was thought to be on AxR1—but in fact turned out to be on St. George, and at over forty years old, the vines today are some of the oldest in the valley. When Chateau Montelena planted vineyards in 1974, they tried to do the conventional thing and use AxR1, but it was in so much demand they couldn't get any, so they used St. George. "We were lucky rather than smart," Bo Barrett recalls happily. A side effect of the replacement of

At the start of the cult wine phenomenon, many small producers shared a tasting room at the Napa Wine Company in Oakville, indicated by the sign to Cult Wine Central

AxR1 since the nineties has been an increase in ripeness; the new rootstocks encourage lower yields and more rapid ripening.

Replanting as the result of the AxR1 debacle forced attention on the selection of the cultivar as well. Clones attract more attention in Napa Valley than perhaps anywhere else that focuses on Cabernet Sauvignon. Until the early nineties, there was little choice, but then the French ENTAV clones from Bordeaux became available as well as the so-called heritage clones that had been propagated from vines previously grown in California. The question about the move towards the ENTAV clones is whether material that was selected in a relatively cool period in Bordeaux will necessarily give the best results in Napa's warmer and drier climate.

The Rise of Cult Wines

The nature of the high end has changed since Napa started concentrating on Cabernet. In 1974, many of the top wines were "Reserves," coming from Beaulieu, Mondavi, or Louis Martini. "Reserve really didn't mean much, although the term was popular at the time. Benziger destroyed the use of the term by making a bulk wine. I always resented that. It was quite different from Estate but even that has been diluted now," says Richard Arrowood, one of the first winemakers to focus on single vineyard wines (in Sonoma).

Today the top wines tend to come from single vineyards, often enough carrying the name of the sub-AVA in which they are located. (However, worried about possible dilution of identity, Napa Valley vintners sponsored a law in 1990 that all wines attributed to any AVA within Napa should in addition mention Napa Valley.) Is the switch in emphasis from reserve bottlings to single vineyards a mark of a maturing wine region?

Although there is a definite move towards single vineyards, there are still some leading wines based on barrel selections. It may be true that single vineyards become more interesting at very small production levels, but blending produces more complexity at higher levels. "Separate vineyard wines from the mountains and valley would be like putting handcuffs on us. Not all lots turn out great every year and quality bounces around the valley like a ball. There's wide variation in sources from year to year. In a cool year, St Helena and Calistoga make the best lots, in a warm year it's Napa and the hillsides," says Chuck Wagner, explaining that Caymus Special Selection is usually a blend of one quarter from mountain sources and three quarters from the valley.

"A cult wine is a wine that you hear all about but never get to taste" is not a bad definition. There have always been wines recognized as *hors de classe*, of course, but the first growths of Bordeaux, and top Burgundies such as Domaine de la Romanée Conti, are available in the marketplace, even if very expensive. The cult wines of Napa are a more artificial phenomenon, often not for sale in general distribution and available only by an allocation to private customers for which there is a long waiting list. They are expensive: the situation is captured by a quote from a producer in 2006: "On several occasions we have had difficulty selling wines at $75, but as soon as we raise the price to $125 they sell out and get put on allocation."

Reputation may depend either on the producer's name or the vineyard. Often enough the same consultants are involved: David Abreu, Heidi Barrett, Helen Turley, Philippe Melka, Michel Rolland, all known for managing vineyards for low yields, or winemaking for high extraction. Their names give instant credibility to new ventures to create cult wines.

Some producers set out from the start to produce only cult wines, using a combination of extreme methods of viticulture and vinification (not unlike the creation of garage wines in Bordeaux) to produce very intense wines. Screaming Eagle is often credited with starting the phenomenon with its inaugural 1992 vintage. Within three or four years, Araujo, Bryant, Colgin, and Harlan followed with the explicit intention of repeating the phenomenon. Now there are many more.

Some vineyards have acquired cult reputations, such as Beckstoffer's various plots in To-Kalon. Those producers who can afford to purchase the grapes produce small quantities of wine at high prices that often achieve cult status. Schrader was one of the first to start the bandwagon by producing a variety of very limited-production runs from different parts of the vineyard.

AVA	Producer	Cuvée
Oak Knoll	Trefethen	Cabernet+ Sauvignon
Stags Leap	Shafer	One Point Five
Oakville	Robert Mondavi	Oakville
Rutherford	Inglenook	"1882" Niebaum-Coppola
St. Helena	Nickel & Nickel	Hayne Vineyard
Calistoga	Chateau Montelena	Sauvignon
Mount Veeder	Mayacamas	Cabernet Sauvignon
Diamond Mountain	Diamond Creek	Gravelly Meadow
Spring Mountain	Pride	Vintner Select
Howell Mountain	Dunn	Howell Mountain
Atlas Peak	Kongsgaard	Cabernet Sauvignon

Reference Wines for Cabernet Sauvignon

When the cult is a vineyard, production is necessarily limited, but in many cases the small production is more a matter of managed scarcity. Production is usually less than 10,000 bottles per year. There is a certain commonality of style to most cult wines: they are almost always dominated by Cabernet Sauvignon, sometimes monovarietal. In many cases, the general policy is "more is better," but it would be naïve to dismiss all cult wines as being monolithic monsters. I do find those that are blends to offer more flavor interest and to age better: Screaming Eagle and Harlan would be good examples.

Prompted partly by the wish to maintain quality (and exclusivity), and partly by difficulties with the economy, the trend to offer second wines accentuated in Napa after the recession of 2008. They have a variety of origins: for cult wines produced in small quantities, they usually come from declassified lots; at larger producers they may represent different sources of material.

The Style of Napa

"Napa Valley is more a concept than a sense of place—it has become a brand and a style in itself," one producer said to me. "Napa Cabernet is the only New World wine ruler that's being used internationally—it wins price, volume, and scores. The reason it's the market winner is because the word *Napa* is a brand," says Leo McCloskey, of Enologix, a company that advises producers on how to increase the impact of their wines in the marketplace.

The question about Napa is to what extent there is uniformity of style, and how important are climate and land as opposed to winemaking? It's probably fair to say that winemaking with Cabernet Sauvignon is less variable than with some other varieties. The most significant factor affecting style is the choice of when to harvest, and certainly the trend towards achieving greater ripeness by later harvesting has played to Napa's general strengths: lots of sunshine and not much water. Insofar as there is a common style, it's an emphasis on ripe fruits that is encouraged by the climate.

Napa has come a long way from the era when the Wine Institute (an advocacy group representing producers) used the slogan, "Every year is a vintage year in California." That was behind the belief that persisted through the seventies that wine is made by winemaking. Site location and vineyard management were all but dismissed as relevant factors, and it was assumed that California's climate ensured perfect ripeness every year. "The predominant thinking at the time was that every variety would give good results if planted in a good place," Bill Phelps recalls. Matching terroir to varieties and taking account of climatic variation came later.

Today at top producers there is more concern to represent the terroir, and recognition that each vintage is different. Indeed, there's a certain disdain at the top Napa producers for technological advice from graduates of the Enology Department of the University of California, Davis. "Graduates from Davis know how to take care of chemicals and things," Fred Schrader says somewhat dismissively. Recollecting Napa's revival, Paul Roberts of Harlan Estate says, "There was the era of students from Davis who came here and said: 'That's how we make wine—going after the correct numbers.' This lasted into the eighties. Today there is more purity and less intervention; we measure numbers but we don't let it drive winemaking." That's the artisanal view.

Alcohol levels have gone up steadily in Napa. In 1975 they were not terribly different from Bordeaux, typically about 12.5% for Cabernet Sauvignon. They increased until peaking around 14.5% in 2004-2208, then declined, and went back up in 2012-2014. Christian Moueix is a bit sarcastic about this. "Remember, before vines arrived in the Napa Valley, there were prunes. The dominant flavor in Napa wines today is prune—it's natural. It's not an unpleasant taste but it's extreme."

Vintages

Vintages have been more erratic since 2000, perhaps a consequence of global warming, but after some real ups and downs ending in the difficult 2011 vintage, there has been a stream of good vintages. "Critics find 2012 to be better than 2014 but I think that's because 2012 followed the miserable 2011 vintage, and 2014 followed the 2013, which is the greatest vintage we've had in fifty years. 2007 and 2010 would be next (after 2013), and then 2014," says winemaker Peter Heitz at Turnbull. In 2017, 2019, and 2020, wildfires created havoc at the end of the season, with the worst damage coming in 2020 when several wineries were destroyed, and yields were reduced by the inability to use grapes with smoke taint. Only about a third of the grapes were harvested before the first fires in August 2020, and some had smoke taint, so overall yield for the year is reduced to about a quarter.

2019		Season started with lots of rain. Long warm summer had even temperatures, cooling trend at end gave good harvest conditions. Large crop expected to produce very high quality wines.	
2018		There's great enthusiasm for this vintage, especially for Cabernet Sauvignon. Temperatures were cooler than usual, but there was continual sunshine. Harvest was up to three weeks later than average. Wines have mid weight structure and tend towards elegance rather than power. Some producers draw a parallel with 2012.	14.6%
2017		Difficult season with rainy periods and alternating temperatures. A heat wave at start of September caused vines to stop development. Wildfires in first week of October were a problem for grapes that had not been harvested. Yields were low.	14.6%
2016	94	Regarded as a perfect growing season giving elegant wines, not as powerful as 2013 or overtly fruity as 2015, but perfectly balanced. A top year for Cabernet. Most people regard 2016 as edging out 2013 as the best year of the decade.	14.9%
2015	93	Very small vintage but rich: flavor is at the forefront here, whereas tannins were at the forefront in 2013.	15.0%
2014	92	Precocious Spring, dry summer, and early harvest gave strong Cabernets, but not as tannic as 2013. Often the most aromatic character of 2012-2014.	14.9%
2013	94	Touted as a great vintage for Cabernet from an ideal season with dry, sunny conditions; the downside is high alcohol. Wines are intense, rich, and muscular: many will require some years to come around. The strong tannins of the vintage are especially evident in Oakville.	15.2%
2012	93	Return to classic conditions with well-structured Cabernets. Very well received with relief after several difficult vintages. Wines can be elegant, without the raw power of 2013.	14.5%
2011	86	A problem vintage because of cool weather and rain, giving lower alcohol levels and lighter wines; difficult to get the right	13.7%

		balance with ripeness. Regarded in the region as poor for reds.	
2010	88	Reduced in size by problems in Spring, with cool conditions followed by heat in late summer. Said to be elegant, but sometimes a bit lacking in character.	14.1%
2009	89	Mild summer, even conditions, wines a bit on lighter side tending to softness for early drinking.	14.5%
2008	90	Reduced in size by Spring frosts, giving concentrated wines that may take time to come around.	14.8%
2007	94	Lush, opulent wines in Napa's modern style, well received and universally praised.	14.7%
2006	90	Slightly lighter vintage that did not attract much attention.	14.8%
2005	92	Cooler, longer growing season gave structured wines. The question is whether fruits will outlive tannins in the long run.	14.5%
2004	91	Early harvest resulted from heat in August. Big, rich wines, maturing relatively early.	14.9%
2003	88	Irregular conditions with cool growing season followed by hot September, generally for drinking early.	14.4%
2002	92	Classic in the new Napa style tending to richness and opulence.	14.6%
2001	93	Even, long growing season gave well-structured wines thought to be long-lived, but I find them a bit lacking in generosity.	14.3%
2000	86	Summer heat waves followed by October rains gave tight acidic wines that were not very well received.	13.8%

Vintages are rated on 100 point scale. Fourth column shows average alcohol in Napa Cabernets.

Visiting the Region

Napa Valley has changed enormously since the start, when there were sporadic wineries up and down route 29, and a few on the Silverado Trail, and you could stop in almost anywhere for a tasting. Today the wineries are choc a bloc, and on a long weekend or during peak summer, the road can be jammed by limos out from San Francisco for the day.

Virtually all wineries sell wine at the cellar door; indeed, for smaller, high-end producers, this represents the majority of sales. Most wineries have tasting rooms, and most now make a charge for tasting. This varies from a nominal cost ($10-20) to cover the   wine being poured to something more significant, especially for special bottlings. (The average charge in Napa is $40.) The profiles show the *minimum*

Downtown Oakville consists of the Oakville Grocery

charge for a tasting. Many wineries offer a variety of tastings at increasing price levels depending on the number and age of wines being poured. Sometimes any charge is credited back if you make a purchase.

Many wineries require an appointment: this usually results in a more extended visit, typically from 60 to 90 minutes, starting with a tour of the vineyards and winery, concluding with a tasting. Typically the charges here are higher, and the visit is regarded as a profit center for the winery. It's usually adequate to make appointments a week or so ahead, but a month or so in advance is a good idea for busy periods. (The cellarpass online system at is used to make reservations for many wineries: see www.cellarpass.com.)

Pressure for appointments is created by restrictions limiting how many visitors a winery is allowed to receive each day. It is fair to say that the atmosphere has become much more commercial in Napa Valley in recent years. It's still possible to drive up the valley and stop to taste without an appointment, but unfortunately this excludes many of the more interesting producers.

Downtown Napa is a bit south of most wineries, although it takes only about 30 minutes to drive up to Calistoga at the northern end of the valley (somewhat longer on busy week-

If there is a center to Napa Valley, it's St. Helena.

At the north end of the valley, Calistoga, formerly famous for its hot springs, is now a tourist destination.

ends or during rush hour). Yountville is a central base for visiting wineries all along the valley, and has several hotels and restaurants, as does St. Helena, towards the northern end. Between Yountville and St. Helena, the Oakville Grocery on route 29 is a good spot to grab lunch. The restaurant scene for fine dining is less interesting than it used to be, as several top restaurants from Yountville to St. Helena have closed due to difficulties.

It's generally less crowded driving along the Silverado Trail than along route 29. Allow much more time for visiting wineries either to the west or to the east of the valley proper, as roads are narrow, steep, and winding.

Many of the wineries in Napa and Sonoma have wine clubs, and may give preference to members for visits, as well as making certain wines available only to them by mail order. It is now also common for wines that are made only in small amounts to be available only at the winery. A typical pattern would be for an AVA wine to be in general distribution, but for single vineyard wines to be available only at the winery or through the wine club.

Maps

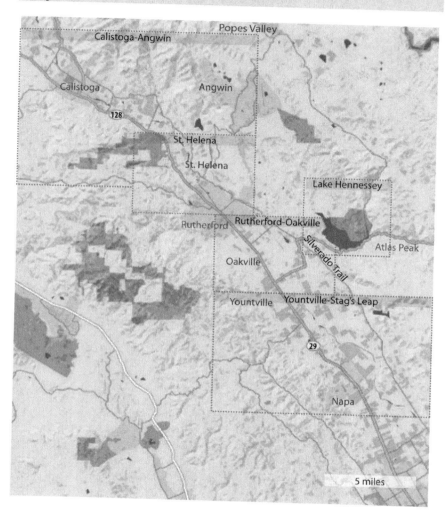

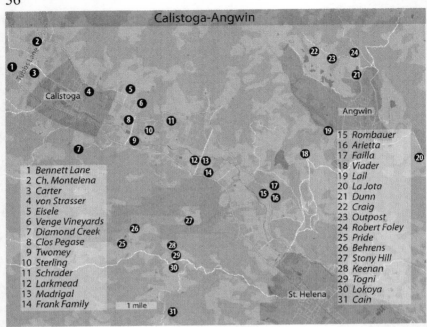

Calistoga-Angwin

Calistoga

Angwin

St. Helena

1 mile

1 Bennett Lane
2 Ch. Montelena
3 Carter
4 von Strasser
5 Eisele
6 Venge Vineyards
7 Diamond Creek
8 Clos Pegase
9 Twomey
10 Sterling
11 Schrader
12 Larkmead
13 Madrigal
14 Frank Family

15 Rombauer
16 Arietta
17 Failla
18 Viader
19 Lail
20 La Jota
21 Dunn
22 Craig
23 Outpost
24 Robert Foley
25 Pride
26 Behrens
27 Stony Hill
28 Keenan
29 Togni
30 Lokoya
31 Cain

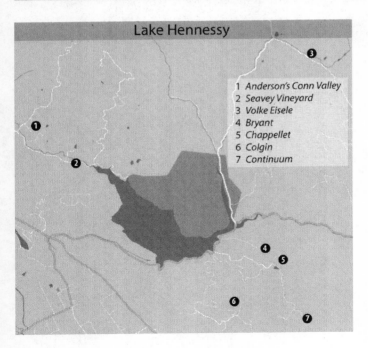

Lake Hennessy

1 Anderson's Conn Valley
2 Seavey Vineyard
3 Volke Eisele
4 Bryant
5 Chappellet
6 Colgin
7 Continuum

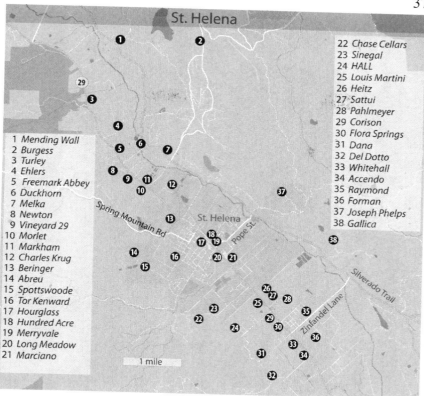

St. Helena

22 Chase Cellars
23 Sinegal
24 HALL
25 Louis Martini
26 Heitz
27 Sattui
28 Pahlmeyer
29 Corison
30 Flora Springs
31 Dana
32 Del Dotto
33 Whitehall
34 Accendo
35 Raymond
36 Forman
37 Joseph Phelps
38 Gallica

1 Mending Wall
2 Burgess
3 Turley
4 Ehlers
5 Freemark Abbey
6 Duckhorn
7 Melka
8 Newton
9 Vineyard 29
10 Morlet
11 Markham
12 Charles Krug
13 Beringer
14 Abreu
15 Spottswoode
16 Tor Kenward
17 Hourglass
18 Hundred Acre
19 Merryvale
20 Long Meadow
21 Marciano

Spring Mountain Rd

St. Helena

Pope St.

Silverado Trail

Zinfandel Lane

1 mile

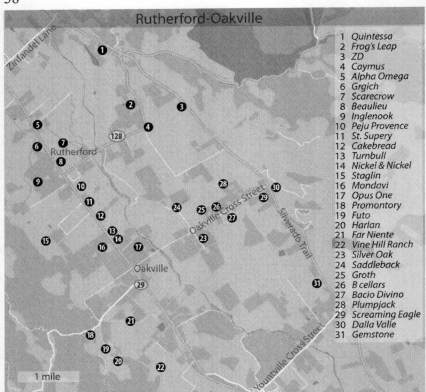

Rutherford-Oakville

1 Quintessa
2 Frog's Leap
3 ZD
4 Caymus
5 Alpha Omega
6 Grgich
7 Scarecrow
8 Beaulieu
9 Inglenook
10 Peju Provence
11 St. Supery
12 Cakebread
13 Turnbull
14 Nickel & Nickel
15 Staglin
16 Mondavi
17 Opus One
18 Promontory
19 Futo
20 Harlan
21 Far Niente
22 Vine Hill Ranch
23 Silver Oak
24 Saddleback
25 Groth
26 B cellars
27 Bacio Divino
28 Plumpjack
29 Screaming Eagle
30 Dalla Valle
31 Gemstone

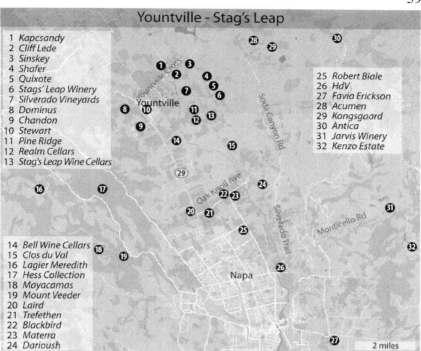

Yountville - Stag's Leap

1 Kapcsandy
2 Cliff Lede
3 Sinskey
4 Shafer
5 Quixote
6 Stags' Leap Winery
7 Silverado Vineyards
8 Dominus
9 Chandon
10 Stewart
11 Pine Ridge
12 Realm Cellars
13 Stag's Leap Wine Cellars

25 Robert Biale
26 HdV
27 Favia Erickson
28 Acumen
29 Kongsgaard
30 Antica
31 Jarvis Winery
32 Kenzo Estate

14 Bell Wine Cellars
15 Clos du Val
16 Lagier Meredith
17 Hess Collection
18 Mayacamas
19 Mount Veeder
20 Laird
21 Trefethen
22 Blackbird
23 Materra
24 Darioush

Napa

2 miles

Profiles of Leading Estates

Ratings	
***	Excellent producers defining the very best of the appellation
**	Top producers whose wines typify the appellation
*	Very good producers making wines of character that rarely disappoint

Symbols

⌖	Address	☺	Tasting room with especially warm welcome
☎	Phone		
	Owner/winemaker/contact	🚶	Tastings/visits possible
@	Email	🗓	By appointment only
🌐	Website	⊘	No visits
◉	AVA	🏭	Sales directly at producer
🍷 Red 🍶 White Reference wines			No direct sales
②	Second wine		Mailing list only
🚜	Conventional viticulture	✖	Winery with restaurant
🍃	Sustainable viticulture		
🌿	Organic		
◓	Biodynamic		

ha=estate vineyards

bottles=annual production

Abreu Vineyards

 2366 Madrona Ave, St. Helena, CA 94574

 +1 707 963 3465

 Brad Grimes or Nicole Burns

 info@abreuvineyard.com

⊕ *www.abreuvineyards.com*

St. Helena

⚑ *Madrona Ranch, Cabernet Sauvignon*

🚫 @ 🍇 🍂

82 acres; 12,000 bottles [map p. 37]

David Abreu has long been famous as a grape grower. Many producers will tell you proudly that a cuvée comes from one of the Abreu vineyards, and Abreu grapes are behind a fair number of Napa's cult wines. Abreu has four properties, and he now keeps grapes from 20-25 acres for making his own wine.

It's hard to describe the mode of viticulture. "I don't keep up on all of the nomenclature around the different farming styles," says Brad Grimes. "We are not certified in any style of farming nor would we ever choose to define ourselves by one or all of those names. I can definitely say that we are unlike any other farming company...We farm all of our vineyards using organic materials, and, at Madrona Ranch, use a circular system of farming that incorporates animals that is more along the lines of biodynamic, although we are not following a manual. So, all of the [categories], with the exception of conventional. That is one thing we are not..."

The facility is a long branching tunnel into the hill, dug in 1979, extended in 1982, then finished in 2006. All the wine is made here in a long row of 2 ton fermenters. There's 100% new oak, 2-3 rackings, no fining: "no reason to fine at all," says winemaker Brad Grimes. Lots are picked when ready and then cofermented irrespective of variety. "One of the advantages of cofermentation is that you can usually balance out acid and alcohol. People tend to think that separating into lots and fermenting as such is more precise, instead of taking fruits that are ready together."

Each of the vineyards—Madrona (23 acres), Capella (6 acres), Thorevilos (20 acres), and Las Posadas (35 acres) on Howell Mountain—has all the Bordeaux varieties. Madrona Ranch in St. Helena is the most famous of the holdings, unusual for its red strip of ferrous soil. There's 65-70% Cabernet Sauvignon at Capella, 45-60% at the others, and some Malbec at Howell Mountain. There's extensive picking—6 passes through Madrona and 3-4 through the other vineyards—and lots that don't make it into the vineyard wines go into a general blend; below that it's sold off in bulk. "I don't get inspiration from Napa, I get it from Bordeaux," says Brad.

There are four single-vineyard wines, and also one wine, Rothwell Hyde, that is blended from all the vineyards. Thorevilos is the most approachable, Capella is the most refined, Las Posadas (Howell Mountain) surprisingly soft at first ("Howell Mountain doesn't have to be hard") until the structure kicks in, and Madrona is the most profound and complete ("What you see about Madrona is the beautiful lively backbone.") For me it has the freshness of Cabernet Franc and the backbone of Cabernet Sauvignon. "California in a Bordeaux style," was the comment of a Bordeaux winemaker at a tasting.

Alpha Omega Winery

*

 1155 Mee Ln, Rutherford, CA 94574

📞 *+1 707 963 9999*

Henrik Poulsen

@ *info@aowinery.com*

🌐 *www.aowinery.com*

Rutherford

Napa Cabernet Sauvignon

😊 💲50 🏨 🍷 🚜

10 acres; 180,000 bottles [map p. 38]

ALPHA OMEGA

CABERNET SAUVIGNON
BECKSTOFFER GEORGES III
RUTHERFORD
NAPA VALLEY
2009

A relatively new enterprise, established in 2006, by Robin and Michelle Baggett who had been grape growers at the Tolouse winery in San Luis Obispo, Alpha Omega operates on an unusual basis: its wines do not go into general distribution but are sold almost entirely at the winery or through the wine club or directly to restaurants. Right on route 29, the premises are designed with entertainment in mind, with a large well staffed tasting room and an outside terrace overlooking the vineyards for sitting and tasting.

Aside from the immediately surrounding vineyard of Sauvignon Blanc, all grapes are sourced from growers. With a Swiss winemaker who comes from Bordeaux, and Michel Rolland as consultant, the objective is to produce wines reflecting both European and Californian influences. The focus is on reds, with 18 different cuvées, including eight single vineyard Cabernets (including many from the most famous vineyards of Napa).

I would describe the house style as very rich, full-force Napa, from the Napa Chardonnay, which is full, fat, buttery, and nutty, to the Proprietary Red (a Bordeaux blend, with varieties that change each year but with Cabernet Sauvignon as the major variety), which is smooth and unctuous. The overt juiciness of style for the varietal Cabernets is more reserved because of structure in the background. There's a steady increase in fruit intensity matched by a greater sense of texture from the relatively straightforward Proprietary Red through the more structured Napa Cabernet (which contains some Petit Verdot and Cabernet Franc but no Merlot) to the deeper single vineyard Cabernets (which are monovarietals). The sheer richness of the fruits makes all of the cuvées more or less immediately approachable.

Beaulieu Vineyards

*

📍 *1960 St. Helena Highway, Rutherford, CA 94573*

📞 *+1 707 967 5205*

@ *info@bv-wine.com*

🌐 *www.bvwines.com*

📷 *Rutherford*

🍷 *Private Reserve, Cabernet Sauvignon*

🚶 $15 🍴 🧺 🚜

1099 acres; 8,400,000 bottles [map p. 38]

Perhaps it's no more than sentimental to include Beaulieu in a list of top Cabernet producers, but it has played such a significant role in the history of Cabernet Sauvignon in Napa Valley. After George de Latour established Beaulieu in the historic heart of Rutherford, the Private Reserve was one of a mere handful of top quality wines made in Napa Valley. André Tchelistcheff, who made the wine from 1938 until his retirement in 1973, became a legend. Although erratic because there were two bottlings, one brilliant and one not so good, the 1974 was one of the top wines of that legendary vintage.

Beaulieu turned away from quality under the ownership of Heublein, beginning its expansion into the broader market; sold on in 1987, became just one of Diageo's labels. Then in 2015 it was sold to Treasury along with most of Diageo's wineries. The tasting room is in a historic building, but the modern winery behind more resembles an oil refinery. However, there are now plans to move production of all but the very top-end wines to Treasury's main winery at Beringer just north of Napa. Perhaps it's an indication of where the focus now lies that in 2017 Beaulieu announced an important initiative: to introduce new labels emphasizing its position as a Napa "Grand Cru" producer!

The Private Reserve today is a workmanlike Cabernet, but does not have that special refinement of the historic classic vintages. This is not surprising considering that the plots in the To Kalon vineyard that had been part of the great Private Reserves were sold to Andy Beckstoffer (from whom several producers now purchase grapes for bottlings of cult Cabernets). There are several ranges of wines at quality levels extending to the entry-level BV Coastal Estates (named for their origin in the Central Coast). The wines are well made and serviceable.

Bell Wine Cellars

*

◎ *6200 Washington St.,*
   Yountville, CA 94599

☏ *+1 707 944 1673*

○ *Sandra Hewitt Bell*

@ *info@bellwine.com*

⊕ *www.bellwine.com*

▣ *Yountville*

▮ *Napa Valley, Cabernet Sauvignon, Clone 4*

📅 $20 🏭 🍇 🍷 🌿

7 acres; 180,000 bottles
[map p. 39]

After spending the 1980s at Beaulieu Vineyards, Anthony Bell started his own winery in 1991 by producing Cabernet Sauvignon from clone 6 in borrowed facilities, moving into his own winery in Yountville in 1998. His style is to make wines with a European sensibility. He was involved in Beaulieu's project for characterizing different clones of Cabernet Sauvignon, and today he produces monovarietal Cabernet Sauvignons from several different clones, as well as a blend with the classic Bordeaux varieties, and a "claret" that also includes some Syrah and Petite Syrah.

Three barrels for each individual clone give around 900 bottles for each of clones 7, 4, 6, and 337. The wines from clone 7 and clone 4 have similar profiles, but on clone 7 you see the fruits first, and this reverses on clone 4 where you see the herbal influence first. All the wines show an impressive sense of the tradition of Cabernet Sauvignon, but the most striking difference is between clone 337, which shows the most lush character—the Dijon clone of Cabernet Sauvignon, you might say—and clone 6, which has the most traditional austerity. The main focus here is on the 6 cuvées of pure varietal Cabernet Sauvignons, but there are also Merlot, Syrah, Chardonnay, and Sauvignon Blanc.

Beringer Vineyards

★★

🔘 *2000 Main Street, St. Helena, CA 94574*

📞 *+1 707 257 5771*

💻 *Mark Beringer*

@
cs_beringer@beringer.com

🌐 *www.beringer.com*

⬛ *St. Helena*

🍷 *Napa Cabernet Sauvignon*

🥂 *Napa, Luminus Chardonnay*

☺ $25 🏭 🍇 🍾 ⊘

9401 acres; 2,800,000 bottles [map p. 37]

Beringer is the longest continuously operating winery in Napa, founded in 1885 by two brothers from Mainz in Germany (which explains the style of their Victorian mansion, the Rhine house). The original purchase was 175 acres. Beringer accumulated 1,600 acres by 1971, when the family sold the company, which moved through various owners to become part of Treasury wine estates. The wines are made at a industrial-looking winery across the street from the historic house, which is now the tasting room. The winery is now the center for Treasury's high-end production, and makes some of the wines under the Beaulieu and Sterling labels, as well as Chateau St. Jean in Sonoma. (Bulk wines are produced at an even larger winery in Paso Robles.)

Although Beringer now produces around 12 million cases in total, the luxury division accounts for under 300,000 cases, coming from less than a third of the estate vineyards.. "The 300,000 probably take more effort to produce than the 12 million," Mark Beringer says dryly. He is Jacob Beringer's great-great grandson; having previously worked elsewhere, he became winemaker here in 2015. "Coming in here there was an established style that needed to be maintained. We were pioneers in the style of Napa and would not want to tinker with something that is successful, so the way we innovate is to try new styles." he says.

Beringer divides its wines into several series: the top-level series are the Private Reserve (Cabernet Sauvignon and Chardonnay), Single Vineyards (seven Cabernets from sites all over Napa, available only at the winery), and most recently the Distinction Series. The difference between the Private Reserve and the Distinction Series reflects changes at Beringer and in the region generally. "Private Reserve Chardonnay is a big buttery wine with large amounts of oak, from a warm region (Oakville), and goes through full MLF. Luminus (in the Distinction series) was designed to be a counterpart: leaner with much less MLF, emphasizing citrus and floral, more food friendly. This has been a trend for probably ten years. Distinction Cabernet Sauvignon had the first vintage in 2014 and the key to this wine is that we tried to create a Cabernet that is a bit more polished and modern, with bright fruits and high toned characteristics from the oak. Quantum (a Bordeaux blend) is sourced from a lot of the same estates as the Private Reserve Cabernet, but we select the lots that have a broader tannin profile and will be more approachable. We want Distinction to be definitely its own style," Mark explains.

Beringer is big on Knights Valley, and two of its wines from there reflect its stylistic range: the Cabernet Sauvignon is a blend, with broad flavors, but the Reserve represents a pure Cabernet, very fine and precise. Of course, the most famous wine is the Private Reserve Cabernet Sauvignon; "It comes primarily from mountain fruit, it is made to age, and will easily last 25 years," Mark says. It is indeed an enormously powerful wine: personally I would not even start a Private Reserve for ten years, and twenty might be better. The difficulty with Beringer is to decide which style suits you: the power of the Private Reserve, the modernity but more muted character of Distinction, or the precision of the single vineyard Cabernets.

Bryant Family Vineyard ★★★

1567 Sage Canyon Rd., St. Helena, CA 94574

+1 314 231 8066

Tony McClung

info@bryantwines.com

bryantwines.com

St. Helena

Bryant, Cabernet Sauvignon

② DB4

12 acres; 27,000 bottles
[map p. 36]

Don Bryant purchased the land for his vineyard in a striking spot on Pritchard Hill overlooking Lake Hennessey. "I bought the top of a mountain for a home site and decided it would be fun to start a vineyard. I looked for the best vineyard within 10-15 miles of the house. There was a vineyard close by, planted with Cabernet Sauvignon and Chardonnay, and run down. All the old winemakers said it was the best vineyard around. Grapes had previously been sold to Caymus and others. I made an unsolicited bid in 1986 for 12 acres, and closed the deal within 24 hours," he recalls.

The first vintage was in 1992, with Helen Turley as the winemaker. Early vintages were propelled into instant success. Since then, there have been several winemakers, with changes in style depending on using techniques ranging from barrel fermentation to greater maceration and extraction. "Helen's wines were very reflective of vintage, perfumed and delicate in 1996, massive in 1997," says a later winemaker, Helen Keplinger.

The vineyard is on west-facing volcanic soils, with a cooling influence from the lake just below. It is divided into 22 blocks spread out over 12 acres, and is planted exclusively with Cabernet Sauvignon (a mixture of Spottswoode clone and 337). The character of Bryant is maintained by declassifying lots into a second wine, called DB4. "Wines that are declassified to DB4 are less concentrated, and the tannins are less refined. DB4 is not necessarily shorter lived than Bryant," says Helen Keplinger. Both Bryant and DB4 are 100% Cabernet Sauvignon, and the latest development is an extension into a Bordeaux blend, called Bettina after Don's wife, coming from David Abreu's vineyards at Madrona Ranch, Thorevilos, and Lucia Howell Mountain; the inaugural vintage is 2009. Bettina is produced in roughly the same quantity as Bryant (around 1,500 cases).

Cakebread Cellars *

📍 *8300 St. Helena Highway, Rutherford, CA 94573*

📞 *+1 800 588 0298*

👤 *James Howard*

@ *cellars@cakebread.com*

🌐 *www.cakebread.com*

⬤ *Rutherford*

🍇 *Anderson Valley, Two Creeks Vineyard Pinot Noir*

🍇 *Napa Valley Cabernet Sauvignon*

🍾 *Carneros, Reserve Chardonnay*

1200 acres; 1,800,000 bottles [map p. 38]

Cakebread Cellars

1992

RUTHERFORD RESERVE
NAPA VALLEY
CABERNET SAUVIGNON

PRODUCED AND BOTTLED BY CAKEBREAD CELLARS
RUTHERFORD, CALIFORNIA, USA
ALCOHOL 14.1% BY VOLUME

Cakebread cellars started more or less by accident when Jack and Dolores Cakebread bought a 22 acre ranch in Rutherford in 1972. The first wine was the 1973 Chardonnay, with only 157 cases produced. The first Cabernet was the 1974 vintage. The winery was built in 1974 and enlarged in 1977; it was replaced by a new building in 1980, and has been continuously expanded ever since. By 1979 the family became fully professionally involved when Bruce Cakebread joined with a degree in oenology from UC Davis. A continuing program of vineyard purchases expanded production into Carneros, Howell Mountain, and Anderson Valley. Estate vineyards provide about 60% of all grapes. There are about twenty wines in all, but the flagship remains Napa Valley Chardonnay, which is half of production; with another 30% in Napa Sauvignon Blanc, Cakebread is largely white wines.

Aside from the Napa Valley bottlings, Chardonnay comes from Carneros, Pinot Noir comes from Anderson Valley, and Cabernet Sauvignon comes from Howell Mountain. There used to be both Pinot Noir and Chardonnay from both Carneros and Anderson Valley, but "The Pinot Noir was exceptional from Anderson Valley and the Chardonnay was just good," says winemaker Julianne Laks, "so now we've focused on one place for each variety." The style for Chardonnay limits MLF, typically to less than a third, but compensates by barrel fermentation followed by battonage to increase texture; it becomes richer going from the Napa to Carneros to the single vineyard Cuttings Wharf. New oak is under a third. "We've always done this with whites, I'm really pleased we stood our ground, people are coming back to our style," Julianne says. I would describe it as a halfway house between the full, rich style of the past, and the more angular style of some recent Napa Chardonnays. The Pinot Noirs show quite an earthy style for Carneros.

The Napa Cabernet has a refined texture, and the sense of precision increases in the Dancing Bear Ranch cuvée from Howell Mountain; the most powerful Cabernet is Benchland Select, a barrel selection from two vineyards in Oakville and Rutherford. A sense of moderation typifies the house, with an effort to keep alcohol down. "We've been very successful with whites by growing the grapes to get maturity at lower Brix. With red grapes it's more difficult. It's not fun making wine with too much alcohol," Julianne says.

Caymus Vineyards

*

8700 Conn Creek Road, P.O. Box 268, Rutherford, CA 94573

+1 707 967 3010

Lynda Sakai

info@wagnerfamilyofwine.com

www.wagnerfamilyofwine.com

Rutherford

Special Selection

$50

74 acres; 360,000 bottles [map p. 38]

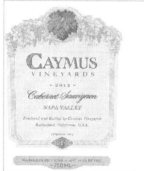

The Wagners have been involved in growing grapes in Napa for a long time. "Napa was a different place when we started in the 1880s, then we had phylloxera and Prohibition, and that put the family out of the business. They planted a litany of crops, the best was prunes, so I grew up around prunes and prune dehydration. In 1966 my father pulled up the prunes and planted grapes," recalls Chuck Wagner.

Caymus Vineyards started in 1972 with a release of 240 cases of Cabernet Sauvignon. Today Wagner has expanded into a group of family businesses, with vineyards and wineries all over Napa Valley. At Caymus there are two Cabernets: the Napa Valley bottling and Special Selection, which has been made most years since 1975 by selecting about a quarter of the best lots. Special Selection can come from any of the eight AVAs in which Caymus own or lease vineyards. It's usually 25% from mountain areas and 75% from the valley, but there's wide variation in sources depending on annual conditions. The style changed in the late nineties to become riper and richer, and since 2008 has included about 15% Merlot. Unlike some of the prominent Napa Valley Cabernets, Special Selection is made in good quantities, typically around 15,000 cases.

House style is definitely on the rich side. Caymus Napa Cabernet shows strong aromatic overtones of high-toned fruits, but when you go to Special Select, the aromatics become less obtrusive but the intensity on the palate deepens. Caymus is rich but Special Select is smoother and deeper. The Wagners also make Conundrum, which started as an entry-level white wine, blended from several varieties, sourced all over California; more recently a red has been added, made in a crowd-pleasing style that's very different from Caymus. There's also a Napa Valley Zinfandel.

Domaine Chandon Winery   *

1 *California Drive, Yount-ville, CA 94599*

☎ *+1 707 944 2892*

@ *customerservice@chandon.com*

⊕ *www.chandon.com*

◉ *Yountville*

🍷 *Etoile*

☺ ☐ ♨ 🍇 ♨

998 acres; 6,000,000 bottles
[map p. 39]

Moët & Chandon have expanded out of Champagne to establish subsidiaries in all corners of the globe. The first Chandon Estate was created in Argentina (1960), followed by Napa Valley (1973), Brazil (1973), Australia (1986), Nashik (India, 2013), and Ningxia (China, 2013). The Napa estate is located just outside of Yountville and was one of the first wineries in the area to make tourism a focus, with a tasting room and high-flying restaurant (now closed to make room for expanding the tasting room).

Chandon has 135 acres of vineyards around the winery, another vineyard on top of Mt. Veeder (overlooking the town of Napa) at 1,800 ft elevation, and 800 acres in Carneros. The focus is on the classic varieties of Champagne, Pinot Noir, Pinot Meunier, and Chardonnay. Initially there was basically a standard Brut and a special cuvée, Etoile, but now there are also rosé, Blanc de Noirs, Blanc de Blancs, single-vineyard wines, and some limited editions. There is no vintage-dated wine in distribution, but small runs from individual years are available at the winery (together with some other small production wines). Still wines are about 10% of sales. The style is richer than Champagne, a little softer and plumper.

Chappellet Vineyard

**

1581 Sage Canyon Road,
St. Helena, CA 94574

+1 707 286 4219

Philip Corallo-Titus

@
concierge@chappellet.com

www.chappellet.com

St. Helena

Signature

101 acres; 360,000 bottles
[map p. 36]

Chappellet is venerable as one of the first wineries to be built in Napa after Prohibition, in 1967 (one year after Mondavi). Driving up the narrow access road from Lake Hennessy, deep into the woods, it feels quite inaccessible. Vineyards aren't visible until you go around to the back of the pyramid-like winery. Covering 700 acres, the estate extends well beyond the vineyards, which range from 1000 to 1700 feet, just above the fog line. Grapes are also purchased from some neighboring vineyards. There were already vines on the property when it was purchased, but they were mostly Chenin Blanc. Following a replanting program in the nineties, most of the vineyard today is Cabernet Sauvignon.

There are two distinct Cabernet Sauvignons: Signature and Pritchard Hill. "The style has evolved but the goal has always been to make bold, fruity, wine. Signature was really designed to be ready; it has as much structure as any Cabernet to age, but we do try to reign in the tannins rather than have a heavy brooding style," says Ry Richards. "Pritchard Hill has a different stylistic objective: more extract, bigger tannins, pure black fruit, boysenberries, espresso coffee, a higher density overall." Signature, which uses 50% new oak, comes from the estate and east-facing hillsides in the vicinity; Pritchard Hill, with 100% new oak, is based on selection, and has been an estate wine from 2012. Both wines used to be 100% varietal but now are blends with just over 75% Cabernet Sauvignon; both also have Petit Verdot and Malbec, but there is Merlot only in Signature. There are 7,000 cases of Signature and 1,500 cases of Pritchard Hill. Beyond Cabernet, there's a full range of wines, mostly varietals.

Chase Family Cellars

*

2252 Sulphur Springs Ave, St. Helena, CA 94574

+1 707 963 1284

Alise Merritt

chase@chasecellars.com

www.chasecellars.com

St. Helena

St. Helena Zinfandel Reserve

$35

15 acres; 20,000 bottles [map p. 37]

BOURN

Hayne Vineyard Zinfandel

A residential street in St. Helena opens out at the end to reveal the Hayne vineyard, with Chase located in a house right at the edge. There is no sign, just a street number. The vineyard dates from 1872, and is now is divided into three parts owned by different members of the Hayne family. Chase has a 12 acre parcel of old Zinfandel, with vines up to 115 years old. Katie Hayne Simpson is the fifth generation owner. "Zin is the heart of Chase. For a family of this size to hold the old Zinfandel vines instead of planting high priced Cabernet Sauvignon is a passion play," she says.

Zinfandel is the core, but Chase also produces Petite Syrah from Calistoga and Cabernet Sauvignon from Stags Leap. The Hayne vineyard is dry farmed, and the vines are head pruned so there is essentially no canopy management. The side exposed to the morning sun is picked several days after the side exposed to afternoon sun (young vines—which means 35 years old—are harvested separately). The morning side has more energy and less alcohol and becomes the Reserve; the afternoon side becomes the Estate wine. The Estate Zinfandel is typical of the variety, with sweet high-toned aromatics, but the Reserve reaches a higher level. "This is the soul of Zin, you get the spice with the purity of fruits," says winemaker Russell Bevan. Its pure fruits are virtually unencumbered by tannins, but it does not go over the top, and is as close to elegance as Zinfandel gets.

The house style here shows refinement and purity; tannins aren't suppressed by powerful fruits but are so fine they recede into the background. This comes from what Russell calls aggressive winemaking. "Everything is pressed while still sweet and finishes fermentation in barrel. The switch is based on tasting tannins, when the wine has reached the level of phenolic extract we want, and there's sufficient flavor." Wines are intended to be consumed on release: "We're crafting wines that are approachable at young age, we give you wines that have verve and energy, so why not enjoy while they are young."

Colgin Cellars

**

🌀 *220 Long Ranch Road, St. Helena, CA 94574*

📞 *+1 707 963 0999*

💬 *Ann Colgin or Paul Roberts*

@ *info@colgincellars.com*

🌐 *www.colgincellars.com*

⬤ *St. Helena*

🔺 *IX Estate*

🚫 @ 🍇 🍃

35 acres; 40,000 bottles
[map p. 36]

CABERNET SAUVIGNON NAPA VALLEY

colgin

2010

TYCHSON HILL VINEYARD

One of the estates that created the cult wine movement, Colgin started with the 1992 vintage of Cabernet Sauvignon from the Herb Lamb vineyard (on the outskirts of Howell Mountain), when Helen Turley sourced the grapes from 14 rows in the most exposed position at the top. Herb Lamb continued to be a signature wine until the vineyard had to be replanted in 2008 (Colgin no longer makes it).

Two other wines come from vineyards around St. Helena. Ann Colgin purchased the Tychson Hill vineyard in 1995, and the first vintage was 2000; located at the north end of St. Helena, it was part of Freemark Abbey (but had collapsed during Prohibition and never been replanted). This is almost pure Cabernet Sauvignon. There's also the Cariad Bordeaux Blend, about half Cabernet Sauvignon, produced since 1999 from a blend between David Abreu's Madrona Ranch and Thorevilos vineyard.

The IX Estate on Pritchard Hill, where all wine is now made, was purchased in 1998; it takes its name from the fact that it was lot #9 on Long Ranch Road. It was planted with a traditional Bordeaux mix of varieties, with about two thirds Cabernet Sauvignon; the estate of 80 ha has 8 ha of vineyards, planted on east-facing slopes to catch the morning sun. The first vintage was 2002. In addition to the IX Estate Bordeaux blend, there's a small amount of Syrah. Focus is exclusively on high-end reds. Production of all wines is small: 1,200-1,500 cases of IX Estate, 250 cases of Tychson Hill, 500 cases of Cariad, and (previously) 500 cases of Herb Lamb.

Some change of style is evident over the years in the direction of greater refinement. Winemaker Allison Tauziet says any difference is due less to changes of vineyard source than to technical advances. "The biggest difference is the increased precision in viticulture. In the early years when we were making wine from Herb Lamb it was very rudimentary in the vineyard and vinification was in a custom crush," she points out. Current vintages are developing slowly: my concern is about the pace at which flavor variety will develop.

The Colgins sold a majority (60%) stake to luxury house LVMH in 2017—LVMH also own Domaine Chandon and Newton—but plan to stay on. Winemaking is not expected to change.

Corison Winery

★★

987 St. Helena Highway, St. Helena, CA 94574

📞 +1 707 963 0826

Cathy Corison

@ mail@corison.com

🌐 www.corison.com

St. Helena

Corison, Cabernet Sauvignon

2 Helios

15 acres; 30,000 bottles [map p. 37]

Cathy Corison has been fascinated with wine ever since she took a wine appreciation course in college; based on French wine, the course defined her reference point as European. She came to Napa in the early seventies and made wine at Chappellet through the eighties. She first made her own wine from purchased grapes, and continued to make wine for other producers until 2003.

The story behind the creation of her winery in Rutherford is that she was determined to find gravelly terroir for her Cabernet Sauvignon, and this turned up in the form of a neglected vineyard in Rutherford. There had been plans to develop the site but they had fallen through. This is the basis for her Kronos Cabernet Sauvignon, with vines (most likely clone 7) that were planted on St. George rootstock about forty years ago. Yields are punishingly low, as not only are the vines old, but the vineyard is infected with leaf roll virus. The extra concentration makes the Kronos Cabernet full and plush.

The Corison Cabernet Sauvignon is a monovarietal bottling, blended from three vineyards in the Rutherford-St. Helena area (some leased, one of which Cathy was recently able to purchase: "It's a big relief to secure the grapes and have complete control," she says). Corison Cabernet tends to come out around 14% alcohol, Kronos is usually closer to 13%. New oak is about 50%.

The latest cuvée is the Sunbasket Vineyard, first vintage 2014. Cathy has been purchasing grapes from the vineyard for 30 years, and recently was able to purchase it. Corison is also leasing four adjacent hectares and replanting them to Cabernet Sauvignon.

Graceful aging is a major stylistic objective. "Aging is very important to me. It's almost a moral imperative to make wines that will have a life," Cathy says. Indeed, the wines age slowly; at a vertical tasting in 2012, my favorite was the oldest in the tasting, the 2001. Since then the style seems to have become richer, as typified by the relatively powerful 2012, but a good acidic backbone keeps this in the tradition of ageworthy Cabernets. Production is about 400 cases of Kronos, and about 2,000 cases of Corison Cabernet. Beyond that, the winery has branched out to offer Cabernet Franc, a rosé from Cabernet Sauvignon, and a Gewürztraminer.

Diamond Creek Vineyards ★★

1500 Diamond Mountain Road, Calistoga, CA 94515

☎ +1 707 942 6926

Phil Ross

@ info@diamondcreekvineyards.com

🌐 www.diamondcreekvineyards.com

Calistoga

🏆 Gravelly Meadow, Cabernet Sauvignon

22 acres; 20,000 bottles
[map p. 36]

Gravelly Meadow

Napa **2001** Valley

Cabernet Sauvignon
grown, produced and bottled on diamond mountain by
DIAMOND CREEK VINEYARDS   CALISTOGA, CA
ALCOHOL 13.5% BY VOLUME

No one had planted vineyards this far north in the mountains when Al Brounstein purchased forested land on Diamond Mountain to create a vineyard in 1968, following a visit to the property with André Tchelistcheff and Louis Martini. Al was not happy with the quality of the Cabernet material that was available in California, but three of the first growths in Bordeaux sold him cuttings, which he then smuggled in by flying privately through Mexico. He was under pressure to plant on AxR1 but stuck to the St George rootstock because it had a good record in the mountains. He intended to emulate Bordeaux, and also planted Cabernet Franc, Merlot, and Malbec for the blend.

There are three individual vineyards, all with roughly the same blend of Cabernet Sauvignon, Merlot, and Cabernet Franc; Petit Verdot comes from a separate plot nearby. Gravelly Meadow is dry farmed, and the other vineyards have irrigation supplied by wells on the property, which has a small lake and a series of waterfalls. All the vineyards were planted at the same time, but Red Rock and Volcanic Hill started producing in 1972, whereas Gravelly Meadow did not produce until 1974. The oldest vines today date from 1988; Red Rock and Gravelly Meadow have more younger vines from a replanting program in the nineties. All vines have been propagated from the original selection, using a nursery on the property. A significant part of the difference between the vineyards is in the tannic structure—taut for Volcanic Hill, elegant for Red Rock, earthy for Gravelly Meadow—so will the characteristic differences between the wines narrow as the tannins resolve with age?

I tasted all three vineyards from 1994 to see whether the differences among current vintages were still evident after twenty years. With the moderate alcohol of the early nineties (12.5%), and delicately balanced palates, these were clearly all food wines, with some convergence in style compared to younger vintages. The fruit spectrum is similar in all three, just a touch more aromatic than you would find in Bordeaux of the period, but there are differences in tannic structure. Volcanic Hill seemed the most mature, savory elements mingling with lightening fruits; Gravelly Meadow seemed the most precise and elegant, a tribute to the conventional wisdom that gravel goes with Cabernet; and Red Rock showed the most evident tannic structure. "Al thought Volcanic Hill would be the longest lived wine, but actually they all age equally well. But Volcanic always comes around last, there is no doubt about that," says Phil Ross. Production is small, around 500 cases each, except for only 100 cases of Lake when it is made. I could not say I have a favorite: in some vintages I prefer Volcanic Hill, and in others Gravelly Meadow. The winery remains committed to exclusively producing Cabernet blends.

With no third generation to carry on, Phil Ross sold Diamond Creek to Roederer in 2020 (following Roederer's acquisition of Merry Edwards in Sonoma the previous year). Roederer also have their long established sparkling wine operation farther north in Anderson Valley . The winemaking team at Diamond Creek is staying on.

Dominus Estate ★★

2570 Napanook Rd,
Yountville, CA 94599

+1 707 944 8954

Tod Mostero

@ info@dominusestate.com

⊕ www.dominusestate.com

Yountville

Dominus

2 Napanook

◈ ⬛ 🍇 ✥

124 acres; 100,000 bottles
[map p. 39]

While a graduate student in oenology at UC Davis, Christian Moueix worked the 1968 vineyard at Beaulieu in Rutherford. In 1982, as owner of Château Petrus in Pomerol, he entered into a partnership to produce wine from the part of the historic Napanook vineyard that was owned by John Daniel's daughter. Since then Moueix has been trying to reconstruct the vineyard in its entirety, and has almost succeeded—there's just a small strip at the top that is still owned by Domaine Chandon. The first release of Dominus, under the aegis of the John Daniel Society, was in 1983. In 1995, Christian Moueix became sole owner of the vineyard, and in 1996 the winery was constructed under the principle that it should blend invisibly into the landscape. It has an unusual double skin, with an outer construction of stones packed into netting hiding the construction inside—in the valley, it's sometimes called the stealth winery.

In 1996, Moueix introduced a second wine, called Napanook after the vineyard, which is produced by declassification. "At this point Dominus became more refined. But Napanook has experienced the same transition over the years towards greater refinement. Napanook is the same wine Dominus was ten years ago, we say among ourselves," says winemaker Tod Mostero. There's no discrimination between the lots up to the point when the wines go into barriques, with the best lots going into new wood; assemblage is nine months later, and Dominus typically gets 40% new oak and Napanook gets 20%. Grapes from a single plot may go into both wines, sometimes coming from opposite sides of the row (harvested separately); Napanook usually comes from the sunny side, Dominus comes from the more restrained shady side.

Dominus usually gives a polished, restrained, impression; it is one of the more restrained Cabernets in Napa. "Over-ripeness is the single most undesirable thing in Napa," says Christian Moueix. Some attitudes come straight from France. "We still make wine that is intended to be aged, you can probably start to drink five years after the harvest, but I consider that it doesn't really begin to become expressive until it's ten years, sometimes twenty," says Tod. Napanook is simpler, more approachable, more obvious. There are 6-7,000 cases of Dominus and 4-5,000 cases of Napanook.

The latest Moueix venture in Napa is Ulysses Vineyard, a property about a mile north of Dominus, purchased in 2008. It is a warmer spot than Dominus. Part of the old Hopper Ranch, the vineyard was being used by Swanson vineyards to produce their Merlot. Moueix replanted the vineyard to Cabernet Sauvignon, with a little Cabernet Franc and Petit Verdot. Made by the Dominus team, the first vintage was 2012.

Dunn Vineyards ★★

805 White Cottage Rd., Angwin, CA 9408

📞 +1 707 965 3642

Mike Dunn

@ ben@dunnvineyards.com

🌐 www.dunnvineyards.com

Howell Mountain

🍷 Howell Mountain, Cabernet Sauvignon

2️⃣ Napa Valley, Cabernet Sauvignon

📅❗ @ 🍇 🍷 🔄

42 acres; 54,000 bottles [map p. 36]

One of the pioneers of Howell Mountain, Randy Dunn identified his vineyard in 1972 when he was winemaker at Caymus. Today it has expanded from the five original acres to about 34 acres planted in a much larger estate. The winery is a practical construction with some equipment outside, and the barrel room tunneled into the mountain. The original vineyard remains the core source for the Howell Mountain grapes, but is due for replanting soon, as yields have dropped significantly. Wine making is traditional; there's very little manipulation, no sorting of the grapes, stems are retained, and pump-overs are vigorous: "We do what we can to extract as much as possible," says Mike Dunn. The only exception is alcohol: Randy Dunn remains adamant that it must be less than 14%.

A program to eliminate Brett, in conjunction with a move to more new oak, lightened the style slightly in 2002. "Before 2002 the optimum age was more than twenty years: now?—give me ten years and we'll see," says Mike Dunn, adding, "I feel the need to repeat that the 'style' hasn't changed except for Brett management, barrel selection, and percent of new barrels." There are two Cabernet Sauvignons: Howell Mountain and Napa Valley. In fact, in a vertical tasting at the winery, my favorite was the Napa 1990. Production is around 3,000 cases of Howell Mountain and 1,200 cases of Napa Valley.

Since 2009, all the estate wine has gone into the Howell Mountain bottling. The Napa Valley bottling included wine from other sources on Howell Mountain as well as from elsewhere in the valley, but from 2009 to 2011 was all Howell Mountain, making it something of a second wine including declassified lots. Since 2012 the estate grapes have been supplemented by purchased grapes from two growers in Coombsville.

Eisele Vineyard Estate ★★

 2155 Pickett Rd, Calistoga, CA

📞 +1 707 942 6061

🖥 Antoine Donnedieu de Vabres

@ wine@eiselevineyard.com

🌐 www.eiselevineyard.com

◉ Calistoga

🍷 Eisele, Cabernet Sauvignon

2️⃣ Altagracia

🗓 @ 🍇 🍷

37 acres; 50,000 bottles
[map p. 36]

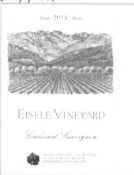

At the northern end of the valley, within a protected canyon east of Calistoga, the Eisele Vineyard has a distinguished history. It was first planted as a vineyard in 1886; Cabernet Sauvignon was planted in 1964. The vineyard is named for the Eisele's, who owned it in the 1970s and 1980s. Paul Draper of Ridge Vineyards made the first commercial release in 1971; this was the one and only vintage of Ridge Eisele. In 1972 and 1973 the grapes were sold to Mondavi (reportedly for the Reserve Cabernet Sauvignon). In 1974, Conn Creek Winery produced the second vineyard-labeled release, and then from 1975 the grapes were sold to Joseph Phelps, who produced a vineyard-designated wine until 1991.

After the property was purchased by Bart and Daphne Araujo in 1991, they made the wine at the estate under the Araujo label. It's difficult to compare the Cabernet from Eisele before and after 1991 given vintage variation and differences in age, but it's interesting that in the one year that both Phelps and Araujo released an Eisele bottling, the wines today show more similarities than differences. The Araujo shows more complex, attractive fruits and is more open; the style of the Phelps is more reserved (in line with earlier Eisele vintages and with their Insignia blend of the period). A savory aromatic thread, somewhat reminiscent of the French garrigue, runs through both wines, giving an impression that the vineyard is expressing its terroir.

The vineyard was heavily virused so the Araujos started an extensive replanting program, but the virusing prevented using selection massale. However, some years earlier, Shafer's home vineyard had been planted with cuttings from Eisele, and Shafer returned the favor with cuttings that were propagated to make the "young" Eisele selection. Cuttings from Eisele were later cured of viruses, and became the "old" Eisele selection. After twenty years, the original vines are now being replanted.

Eisele has an unusual terroir. The vineyards are on an alluvial fan coming straight off the Palisades mountains, but they are not very fertile, and fertility decreases going away from the mountain. Going up the slope you get more clay soils and higher vigor, the opposite of the usual order. The property has 70 ha, and 15 ha are planted out of 16 plantable hectares. Cabernet Sauvignon is planted in the most gravelly part of the vineyard, but there are blocks of Merlot, Petit Verdot, Cabernet Franc, Syrah, Sauvignon Blanc, and Viognier. In the early days, the Phelps Eisele was 100% Cabernet Sauvignon, as were the first two Araujo vintages, but since then the wine has been a blend, usually 85-95% Cabernet Sauvignon with some Cabernet Franc and Petit Verdot, sometimes also a little Merlot. Since 1999 there has been a second wine, Altagracia, also based on a Bordeaux blend, but which fluctuates more widely in varietal composition, from 58% to 100% Cabernet Sauvignon.

In 2013, the estate was sold to François Pinault of Château Latour; in 2016 he changed the name from Araujo Estate to Eisele Vineyard Estate. The Araujos started a new venture called Accendo Cellars (see mini-profile), the year after selling the Araujo Estate.

Far Niente

*

 1350 Acacia Dr, Oakville, CA 94562

☎ +1 707 944 2861

Nicole Marchesi

@ info@farniente.com

🌐 www.farniente.com

Oakville

🍷 Martin Stelling Vineyard, Cabernet Sauvignon

🍷 Oakville Cabernet Sauvignon

Napa Chardonnay

274 acres; 500,000 bottles
[map p. 38]

Just across from Martha's Vineyard, Far Niente is an gothic building dating from the mid nineteenth century. Approached by a long, elegant drive, it's surrounded by gardens rather than vineyards. An old property that had fallen into disrepair, it was purchased by Gil and Beth Nickel in 1979. The old stone house was restored; for the first three years wine was made offsite, but in 1982 resumed at the property. The caves underneath the building where the barriques are stored were constructed recently, in stages since 1990. Then in 1997 the Nickels purchased the Sullenger property, also in Oakville, which they renamed as Nickel & Nickel, which focuses on a series of single-vineyard wines. (Some fruit from the John C. Sullenger vineyard goes into Far Niente Napa Cabernet.) A majority stake in both properties was sold to GI Partners, a San Francisco private equity firm, in 2016.

Far Niente focuses on two varietal wines: Chardonnay and Cabernet Sauvignon. "The model is to make one truly great Chardonnay and Cabernet in each vintage," says winemaker Nicole Marchesi. The major source for estate grapes is the Martin Stelling Vineyard, named for a former owner who built up the vineyard, but died before it produced grapes. Located just to the west of the winery, running up to the hills of Oakville, it was planted in 1978 with Cabernet Sauvignon and other Bordeaux varieties. Far Niente has been 100% Oakville since 2001 (production declined when the other sources ceased to be used). The Cabernet Sauvignon is smooth and approachable, with a silky texture. I remember when the Chardonnay used to show a powerful oaky style, but today it is sourced largely from Coombsville and the style is leaner.

Another single vineyard Cabernet will be introduced as the result of the purchase of a 60 acre parcel in Rutherford in 2017. Far Niente also owns Dolce, a property in Coombsville that produces a late harvest wine from a vineyard farmed to encourage botrytis. A blend of Sémillon with Sauvignon Blanc, Dolce is one of Napa's few dessert wines.

Grgich Hills Estate

*

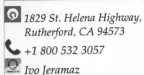

📍 *1829 St. Helena Highway, Rutherford, CA 94573*

📞 *+1 800 532 3057*

👤 *Ivo Jeramaz*

@ *info@grgich.com*

🌐 *www.grgich.com*

▣ *Rutherford*

🍷 *Rutherford Cabernet Sauvignon*

🍾 *Carneros Chardonnay*

😊 💲20 🏭 🍇 🍃

366 acres; 780,000 bottles

[map p. 38]

An immigrant from Croatia who arrived in America with nothing but a small suitcase, Mike Grgich was at Beaulieu during the 1960s, and then gained instant fame as the winemaker who crafted the 1973 Chardonnay at Chateau Montelena that won the Judgment of Paris tasting in 1976. Together with a business partner in 1977, he founded his own winery, Grgich Hills, in Rutherford. His nephew Ivo Jeramaz came from Croatia to help, and to-day Ivo's daughter is involved, so the estate is into the third generation (which however seems short compared to the 15 generations of winemakers back in Croatia).

The estate has an extensive range of vineyards in five locations, all the way from south to north in Napa, in Carneros, American Canyon, Yountville, Rutherford, and Calistoga. "Mike was very smart," says Ivo, "he bought land early and never paid more than $20,000 an acre." The property changed its name to Grgich Hills Estate in 2003 to reflect the fact that since then only estate grapes have been used. "Production went down 40% but we are very happy that we are making better wines," Ivo adds. All vineyards are dry farmed, and farming is intensely organic (in fact basically biodynamic), with a range of birds to eat the insects, and several acres of flower and other plants with bees kept, to avoid the problems of monoculture.

Although Chardonnay was where Mike made his reputation, it is no longer the main focus. "Napa is not known for great Chardonnay any more—there is Chardonnay made everywhere—but Napa has a monopoly on great Cabernet. We used to make more Chardonnay than Cabernet but now it's reversed," Ivo explains. Still there is a hierarchy of Chardonnays: "Napa is the village wine, Carneros (from a single vineyard) is premier cru, and then there is Miljenko's Selection from specific vineyard blocks." The Carneros, perhaps because it has no new oak and malolactic fermentation is blocked, is the most elegant; it ages well for a decade. There are Cabernets from Napa, Rutherford, and Yountville, all moderate in style, but my favorite is Rutherford for its slight aromatic lift. The house style is never over stated.

Groth Vineyards & Winery

★

750 Oakville Crossroad, Oakville, CA 94562

📞 +1 707 944 0290

Suzanne Groth

@ info@grothwines.com

🌐 www.grothwines.com

Oakville

🍷 Oakville Cabernet Sauvignon

Napa Valley, Hillview Vineyard Chardonnay

💲35

161 acres; 860,000 bottles [map p. 38]

Groth is a classic story of a family who moved from elsewhere to start and run a winery in Napa. Dennis and Judy Groth came from computer maker Atari and bought a contiguous block of 120 acres on the valley floor in Oakville in 1981, followed by a smaller property south of Yountville. Production began immediately and increased rapidly, and by 1985 the winery was a full time occupation. The striking pink building (intended to follow the style of the old Missions) was constructed in 1990 and extended in 2007. Michael Weis, now winemaker emeritus, was in charge for twenty years until he handed over to Cameron Parry in 2014.

The Oakville property is planted with Cabernet Sauvignon and Sauvignon Blanc; Merlot and Chardonnay are planted at Yountville. Sauvignon Blanc is the largest production, just ahead of Cabernet Sauvignon: Chardonnay is only about 10%. Groth makes only four wines: the three varietals plus a Cabernet Reserve. The Oakville Cabernet includes grapes from other growers in Oakville, but the Reserve comes only from a specific 27 acre block in the northwest corner of the estate, with soils of sedimentary rocks. "In terms of Oakville, remember that soils vary from clay to alluvial to loess. So the Reserve is a wine of one place, but the Oakville Cabernet is a reflection of everything that is happening in Oakville," says Michael Weis. Although it includes some Merlot, the style emphasizes purity of fruits to give an impression of the penetrating linearity of pure Cabernet Sauvignon. The Reserve is more intense, spicy and chocolaty.

"The Chardonnay comes from the Hillside Vineyard south of Yountville because that region is 15% cooler. Chardonnay from here is not as vibrant as from Yountville. Groth has always made a non-malo Chardonnay, that's the style of the house. Malo adds a dimension to the wine that I don't like, I'd rather have something clean and crisper," Michael says. The Sauvignon Blanc (all from the Oakville estate and local growers, although it is labeled as Napa Valley) is fermented in old barrels and shows a rich style, with exotic fruit notes. The wines offer a good representation of the current character of Napa Valley.

HALL

*

401 St. Helena Highway S, St. Helena, CA 94574

+1 707 967 2626

Steve Leveque

visit@hallwines.com

www.hallwines.com

St. Helena

Rutherford Cabernet Sauvignon

Napa, Kathryn Hall Cabernet Sauvignon

$40

499 acres; 1,200,000 bottles [map p. 37]

The winery in St. Helena stands on a site where wine has been made since 1885; at one time it became a cooperative, and Kathryn Hall purchased it in 2002. Designed for Cabernet production, the glass-sided post-modern winery has fermentation tanks visible through the glass. HALL produces around ten different Cabernet Sauvignons, extending from the Napa Cabernet Sauvignon, which includes a little Merlot and is about a third of production, to wines from individual AVAs or single vineyards. "We source grapes from top vineyards in thirteen of the Napa AVAs," says winemaker Megan Gunderson Paredes, "with about 40% coming from estate vineyards."

There is a focus on vineyard designates, which are generally 100% Cabernet Sauvignon, although there are also wines designed to show the art of blending (more between sources than between varieties). The approachable Napa North End Cabernet is intended to show the juiciness of fruit from the valley north of St. Helena. By contrast, Ellie's Cabernet comes from mountain fruit and is taut and more restrained. New oak is around 75% for the blended wines, and increases to 90% for the single-vineyard wines, which tend to be sterner and to require a few years before drinking.

House style shows an underlying sweetness and refined texture from both valley floor and mountain, but alcohol levels are high, often around or above 15%. "These wines are delicious expressions of their sites, I don't want to put on parameters that will limit them," Megan says. The style is smooth, you might say sleek rather than unctuous. The WALT program, introduced in 2010 to focus on Pinot Noir and Chardonnay, sources grapes from Anderson Valley and Santa Rita Hills as well as Carneros and Sonoma. Another winery is being built at Sebastopol for it. Only ten of the larger production HALL or WALT wines are available in general distribution.

In addition to the facility in St. Helena, where it's possible to walk in, there is also tasting room in Rutherford, requiring appointments, and focusing specifically on the limited-production wines.

Harlan Estate

★★★

1567 Oakville Grade, Oakville, CA 94562

+1 707 944 1441

Summer Jimenez

@ info@harlanestate.com

www.harlanestate.com

Oakville

Harlan Estate

2 The Maiden

40 acres; 32,000 bottles
[map p. 38]

Harlan's two hundred acre estate is a beautiful property in the hills above Oakville, overlooking Martha's Vineyard, To Kalon, and Napanook. After several years searching for land in Napa, Bill Harlan bought the land in tranches, starting in 1984, and planted the vineyards between 1985 and the early 1990s. The estate rises from 200 feet to 1,000 feet, with the vineyards planted up to 500 feet. The original vineyards were planted at 1,800 vines/ha, which was considered a relatively high density at the time, but subsequent plantings have moved up to 5,400 vines/ha, and even 7,500 (positively Bordeaux-like).

The plantings are a classic Médoc mix, about 70% Cabernet Sauvignon, the rest Merlot, Cabernet Franc, and Petit Verdot. About three quarters of the terroir is volcanic, and one quarter sedimentary; Merlot is grown on the sedimentary soils as they have better water retention.

None of the first three vintages (1987-1989) were sold commercially; the first commercial vintage, 1990, was released in 1996. Michel Rolland is the consulting winemaker. A second wine, The Maiden, is about a quarter of production. The wines age well: recently my favorite vintage has oscillated between the 1991 and the 1995.

Together with winemaker Bob Levy, Bill Harlan started a second operation in 1997; BOND (see mini-profile) has the same winemaking team, but here the objective is to produce cuvées that express Cabernet Sauvignon from different terroirs. Bill Harlan's latest project is Promontory (see mini-profile), a new winery in the foothills of Mount Veeder.

Heitz Cellars ⃰

📍 *436 St. Helena Highway,*
  St. Helena, CA 94574

📞 *+1 707 963 3542*

🔑 *Tiffany Egan*

@ *info@heitzcellar.com*

🌐 *www.heitzcellar.com*

🔲 *St. Helena*

🍷 *Trailside Vineyard, Cabernet Sauvignon*

🚶 💲 🏭 🍇 🛢 🥃

425 acres; 480,000 bottles
[map p. 37]

Dating from the 1960s, Heitz is now regarded as one of the venerable old Napa producers. Joe Heitz started as André Tchelistcheff's assistant at Beaulieu in 1951, spent a period running the Department of Enology at Fresno State University, and then returned to the valley to launch Heitz with 8 acres of land along route 29. The original winery is the site of the Heitz tasting room today. The present winery in St. Helena was purchased in 1964, and about 50 acres of vineyards were planted around it. However, the real breakthrough came in 1965 when the Heitz's started buying Cabernet Sauvignon grapes from Tom and Martha May's vineyard in Oakville. Initially the grapes were blended into the general Cabernet bottling, but then Joe decided to make a single-vineyard wine (the first in California). From its first vintage in 1966, Heitz Martha's Vineyard was regarded as a benchmark for Napa Cabernet; the 1974 is still regarded as one of the best wines ever made in California. It was made by Joe's son, David, who is still the winemaker today.

Heitz has always produced an extensive line of varietals, including the Napa Valley Cabernet, Zinfandel, Chardonnay, and Sauvignon Blanc, but none has achieved the acclaim of the single vineyard Cabernets. After the initial years, Cabernet Sauvignon grapes were purchased to augment the supply for the Napa Valley Cabernet, but today the only grapes not coming from the estate itself are those from Martha's Vineyard. In fact, after purchasing the 217 acre Ink Grade Vineyard just east of Howell Mountain, Heitz had surplus grapes to sell.

In addition to its most famous wine, there have been two other single vineyard Cabernets, Bella Oaks (in Rutherford) and Trailside (on the other side of the valley by the Silverado Trail). Like Martha's Vineyard, Bella Oaks belonged to a couple, Barney and Belle Rhodes, who sold the entire crop to Heitz. Production of Bella Oaks stopped in 2007, because the vineyard was sold. The style with the single vineyard Cabernets is for quite extended oak aging, with one year in old foudres of American oak and redwood, followed by thirty months in French barriques, including a high proportion of new oak (usually 60% for Bella Oaks, 70-80% for Martha's Vineyard and 100% for Trailside). Certainly there is a similarity of style, especially between Bella Oaks and Martha's Vineyard, although Martha's Vineyard is always the most intense, and needs the most time to come around. I still don't think any subsequent vintage has equaled the 1974. Rather unusually, Heitz is known for blocking malolactic fermentation in its red wines to maintain freshness.

An infection in the winery with TCA made the vintages from 1985 questionable (the 1987 was the worst affected), and it took several years for the problem to be recognized; the wines did not become completely free of cork taint until 1992. And then the vineyard had to be replanted because of phylloxera, so there was no vintage in 1995; the wine came from relatively young vines for the rest of the decade. Has Martha's Vineyard ever fully recovered its reputation? Some recent vintages suggest a road to recovery; others seem to have lost their way.

For all the ups and downs, Heitz remains an icon in Napa Valley, but was sold in 2018 for $180 million to billionaire Galyon Lawrence, from a family involved in agriculture and industry. A sign of new investment was Heitz's purchase of a 50 acre Cabernet Sauvignon vineyard in Rutherford from Treasury Wine Estates, which was previously part of Sterling Vineyards.

Inglenook

*

1991 St Helena Highway,
Rutherford, CA 94573

+1 707 968 1100

reservations@inglenook.com

www.inglenook.com

Rutherford

Rubicon, Cabernet Sauvignon

☺ $45 🏭 🍇 🌿

326 acres; 3,200,000 bottles
[map p. 38]

The old Inglenook winery at the heart of Rutherford has a chequered history. Some people regard it as the birthplace of fine wine, or at least of fine wine based on Cabernet Sauvignon, in Napa. Finnish sea captain Gustave Niebaum, who made a fortune trading furs in Alaska, decided after a visit to France that the gravelly loam soils of Rutherford resembled Bordeaux and might reward attempts to produce the same blend of wine. He planted Cabernet Sauvignon, together with Cabernet Franc and Merlot. A splendid Gothic mansion was constructed to house winemaking.

Inglenook Cabernets were famous in the period after Prohibition. The winery was sold to United Vintners in 1964, and then became part of Heublein when United Vintners was itself sold in 1969. Quality went out of the window. In 1975, film director Francis Ford Coppola purchased Niebaum's former home together with 49 hectares of surrounding vineyards, and then in 1995 Heublein tired of the business and sold him the Inglenook winery and the rest of the vineyards. The house is now a visitor center, and viticulture and vinification have been modernized. The original holdings were reunited under the name Rubicon Estate. The Inglenook name was sold to Constellation, who sold it to The Wine Group in 2008; it was used for jug wine until Coppola got it back in 2011 (it cost much more than the original purchase of the estate). The estate was also expanded by purchasing other vineyards, including 60 ha from the J.J. Cohn property in Rutherford in 2002.

The winery is now called Inglenook, and the top wine is called Rubicon (a classic blend with about 90% Cabernet Sauvignon). The second wine was previously called CASK, but now is labeled simply as Inglenook Cabernet Sauvignon (it's a similar blend to Rubicon). 1882 is 100% Cabernet Sauvignon, at a lower price point. The wines are quite mainstream for Napa. There's also Syrah, Zinfandel, Sauvignon Blanc, and a Rhône-style white. A new winemaker, Philippe Bascaules, was hired from Château Margaux in Bordeaux in 2011, and is moving the wines in a lighter, more elegant direction.

Francis Coppola also has two wineries in Sonoma, and production of most of the wines under the Inglenook label has been moved to the Francis Ford Coppola Winery. Rubicon is only 60,000 bottles out of the total. Most tourism now goes to Francis Ford Coppola winery in Geyserville (see *Guide to Sonoma*).

Jarvis Winery

  2970 Monticello Rd, Napa, CA 94558

☎ *+1 800 255 5280*

👤 *William Jarvis*

@ *wines@jarvisnapa.com*

🌐 *www.jarviswines.com*

◉ *Napa Valley*

🍷 *Cabernet Sauvignon Reserve*

🗓 💲80 🏭 🌿 🚜

37 acres; 85,000 bottles [map p. 39]

The creation of William Jarvis, whose career was in Silicon Valley, Jarvis has a rather unusual facility, a bunker cut into the mountain (using the equipment that created the Channel tunnel between England and France). The tunnel curves around in a large circle, with rooms off to the side and tanks and vats along the way.

Well to the east of Napa Valley proper, vineyards are at 1,000 foot elevation and are around 6 degrees cooler than the valley floor. There are several separate vineyards occupying 37 planted acres out of a total estate of 1,320 acres. Fermentation is all in stainless steel, with some rotary tanks used for Cabernet Sauvignon and Cabernet Franc. MLF is performed in large wooden vats, then the wine goes into barrels. Production is only estate wine; the first vintage was 1992.

The focus is on Cabernet Sauvignon, using one of the clones that performed best in the trials at Beaulieu, giving low yields. Most of the wines are single varietals, particularly Cabernet Sauvignon, Cabernet Franc, Merlot, and Chardonnay. The Reserve designation is used for the top wines, which are barrel selections. The Lake William cuvée was created by accident when William Jarvis pumped Cabernet Franc into a tank of Cabernet Sauvignon. Consulting winemaker Dimitri Tchelistcheff was very cross, until it turned out that the wine was actually rather successful, and it has now become a regular bottling in the range. The Cabernet Sauvignon has quite a restrained style, the Reserve has more density and chocolate notes, the Lake William actually seems more tightly structured, and the top Chardonnay, Finch Hollow, tends towards the exotic.

Joseph Phelps Vineyards

**

📍 *200 Taplin Road, St. Helena, CA 94574*

📞 *+1 800 707 5789*

👤 *Bill Phelps*

@ *info@josephphelps.com*

🌐 *www.josephphelps.com*

🍷 *St. Helena*

🍷 *Napa Valley, Cabernet Sauvignon*

🍾 *St. Helena, Sauvignon Blanc*

474 acres; 780,000 bottles [map p. 37]

Phelps is one of the most reliable producers in Napa. It has expanded significantly, with vineyards in Sonoma as well as various locations in Napa Valley, and Pinot Noir, Sauvignon Blanc, and Viognier also in its line up, but the heart of the operation remains in Cabernet Sauvignon. Its most famous wine is Insignia.

Insignia is one of California's most genuine cult wines, meaning that it is produced in appreciable quantities (up to 20,000 cases), roughly comparable to a Bordeaux château. As a selection of the best cuvées, it should represent the best of the vintage, but at these quantities should still be strongly influenced by general vintage character. It has been a Cabernet-dominated blend since the 1980s, averaging around 80% Cabernet Sauvignon, with the remainder coming from all the other Bordeaux varieties in varying proportions. The grapes originate in about six vineyard plots, in various parts of Napa Valley. Vintage 2003 was the last year in which any grapes came from growers: today the wine is entirely an estate production.

The wine is not easy to judge when young, given the powerful fruits, which take ten years or more, depending on vintage, to resolve enough to allow complexity to show. I am inclined to divide the Insignias into two series. There's a lineage of vintages 1997, 2001, 2007, which seems more European in balance and restraint; there's an alternative lineage from 1999, 2002, 2008, which shows more overt fruit and aromatics in the New World style. I could not see any direct correlation with varietal composition, which changes in order to maintain consistency of style, and it therefore seems that the differences reflect vintage character, which is as it should be.

Kongsgaard Wine

**

4375 Atlas Peak Road, Napa, CA 94558

+1 707 226 2190

John Kongsgaard

info@kongsgaardwine.com

www.kongsgaardwine.com

Atlas Peak

Napa Chardonnay

25 acres; 36,000 bottles
[map p. 39]

Standing in the winery, a cave tunneled into the mountain, Alex Kongsgaard says, "You're looking at the whole business here, Mom and Dad (John and Maggie Kongsgaard) and the two of us" (Alex and vineyard manager Evan Frazier). Kongsgaard is certainly a small producer. Located just short of the end of the road at the summit of Atlas Peak, at an elevation of 2,200 feet, it is not the most accessible vineyard. The winery is nothing if not discrete, and it's easy to shoot past and end up at the Kongsgaard's residence. The location is a bit off the beaten track from the rest of Atlas Peak, as most vineyards are located on Soda Canyon Road, running parallel on the slopes of the mountain just to the north. John Kongsgaard was winemaker at Newton for fifteen years, and then spent a period at Luna, where he also made his own wines, before moving to Atlas Peak in 2006.

Kongsgaard is most famous for its Chardonnay, The Judge, which comes from a small (5 acre) vineyard on an outcrop between Napa and Coombsville. That property has been in the family for almost a hundred years. "It's basically a rock pile, it was explicitly purchased as a rock pile by my great grandfather who was going to quarry it," Alex explains. That never happened, but a few houses were built, and John Kongsgaard ended up planting a vineyard in what was basically his backyard. "It's a very extreme site. The soil is so poor that if we take a sample to the soil science people, they say it's not possible to grow anything," Alex says. Before John Kongsgaard started bottling it separately, the grapes were sold to Newton and were part of the Unfiltered Chardonnay. Even though the site is small, there's significant variation in the soil, and barrel samples show variation from sweet, ripe citrus-driven, flavors, picked early and put into natural oak, to richer more stone fruits put into new oak. Fermentation is very slow: in February 2017 some lots from the 2016 vintage still had not finished fermentation. It's a powerful, full-flavored wine, but has what would be a sense of tannic restraint if it were a red wine. Alcohol is around 15%: "to us that's the level the wine achieves at the peak of ripeness and flavor development," Alex says. "The Judge pushes towards mineral, but the Napa Chardonnay is more openly expressive, more easily approachable."

The Napa Chardonnay is the flagship wine, the only one in national distribution, mostly sourced from the Hyde and Hudson vineyards in Carneros, although like all the Kongsgaard wines it is labeled as Napa AVA. "John generally takes a dim view of the AVA system as not really being useful to us," Alex explains. The Cabernet has a touch of Merlot in most years; originally grapes came from Abreu, but now come from the home vineyard, which was planted in 2009 and came on line in 2014, and from neighboring vineyards. Other cuvées include a Merlot, the Fimasaurus Merlot-Cabernet blend, and Syrah, but all in very small amounts. The reds are rich and chocolaty, with the Cabernet very pure and deep, Fimasaurus broader, Merlot offering a more uplifted impression, and Syrah nutty and elegant. The wines go on sale in August each year and typically sell out to the mailing list in a few weeks. Then there is no more until the next release.

Larkmead Vineyards

*

1100 Larkmead Lane,
Calistoga, CA 94515

+1 707 942 0167

Laurie Taboulet

info@larkmead.com

www.larkmead.com

Calistoga

Napa Valley Cabernet
Sauvignon

 $100

101 acres; 100,000 bottles
[map p. 36]

One of the oldest wineries in Napa, Larkmead was established in 1873. It was one of the Big Four after Repeal, but the modern era starts from 1987 when production restarted, using a custom crush facility until the new winery was built in 2005. The vineyards are around the winery, right at the northern end of Napa Valley where the Mayacamas and Vaca mountain ranges all but join together. It is a very hot spot in summer. The original winery is a stone house across the street from the modern buildings, where the tasting room is housed in a charming white building; the winery, a practical building with a vat room and two barrel rooms, is just behind.

The focus is on red wine, with a small production of Sauvignon Blanc and Tocai Friulano (actually the oldest vines on the property). The basic red comes from the youngest vines, with the blend depending on the year. The White Label wines are blends that are released in the Spring, and include Firebelle (a Merlot-based blend), Cabernet Sauvignon (the workhorse wine), Lillie (Sauvignon Blanc blend), and LMV Salon (Cabernet Franc blend). The Black Label wines are released later, in the Fall, and come from single plots. Aside from the Tocai, they are all varietal Cabernet Sauvignon, including Dr. Olmo (from a plot of gravel), Solari (from a mix of gravel and clay), and The Lark (from an atypical sandy plot).

The house style is fine and silky, from Firebelle with its slightly higher-toned aromatics, to the smoky Napa Cabernet, the tight Dr. Olmo, and the nutty Solari. The intention is that wines can be enjoyed immediately on release, and certainly the tannins are fine enough not to present an obstacle, but flavor variety is better developed if you wait three or four years after release.

Louis Martini Winery

*

📍 254 St. Helena Highway South, St. Helena, CA 94574

📞 +1 707 963 2736

@ info@louismartini.com

🌐 www.louismartini.com

◉ St. Helena

🍷 Monte Rosso, Zinfandel

😊 $25 🏭 🍇 🍷

679 acres; 1,200,000 bottles
[map p. 37]

One of the oldest established wine producers in California, Louis Martini had its origins when the first Louis started making wine at the beginning of the twentieth century, and somewhat unusually formed his own company during Prohibition to produce sacramental wine and kits for home winemaking. At the end of Prohibition he built a winery in St. Helena. In 1938 he expanded into Sonoma by purchasing the Goldstein Ranch (originally planted in the 1880s), which he renamed Monte Rosso. In 1951 his son, also Louis Martini, took over winemaking, and in 1977 the third generation, Michael Martini, took over. The winery and vineyards were sold to Gallo in 2002. Martini's general production is more or less standard for Napa, but Monte Rosso really is a special representation of Sonoma.

The best known vineyard in Sonoma, Monte Rosso is renowned for both its old Zinfandel and Cabernet Sauvignon. Today there are 25 ha of Zinfandel, 40 ha of Cabernet Sauvignon, and 6 ha of Petite Syrah or other varieties. There are two blocks of white grapes. Martini produces several wines from Monte Rosso. The most famous is probably the gnarly vine Zinfandel, which comes from some of the oldest plantings, followed by the (100%) Cabernet Sauvignon. A special blend called Los Ninos was produced from 1979, initially as a Cabernet, then becoming a Meritage after 1985; the blend included Petit Verdot for the first few years and from 2001 had Cabernet Franc as the other variety. In 2008 Martini introduced a Proprietary Red, which is more than half Petit Verdot with one third Cabernet Sauvignon.

Mayacamas Vineyards

*

1155 Lokoya Road, Napa
CA 94558

+1 707 224 4030

Jimmy Hayes

contact@mayacamas.com

www.mayacamas.com

Mount Veeder

Mt. Veeder Cabernet
Sauvignon

Mt. Veeder Chardonnay

52 acres; 90,000 bottles
[map p. 39]

MAYACAMAS

2008
MT VEEDER · NAPA VALLEY
CHARDONNAY
PRODUCED AND BOTTLED BY
Mayacamas Vineyards
NAPA, CALIFORNIA, U.S.A. ALCOHOL 14½% BY VOLUME

"The road from St. Helena is closed by a mud slide, be sure to come from Oakville," I was warned before I set out for Mayacamas. It may be only 20 minutes from downtown Napa, but driving up the narrow, winding, precipitous road onto Mount Veeder, it feels quite inaccessible, which is all the more surprising as it is one of the older wineries, dating from the nineteenth century. The estate is well up in the mountains at the border of Napa and Sonoma, with vineyards at elevations from 1,800 to 2,400 feet, and views across to San Pablo Bay. The only way to see the vineyards is in an open off-road vehicle; driving through the extended forest, you come to clearings with vineyards. There are 25 individual vineyard plots, at varying elevations and exposures. Soils are varied but generally volcanic; there is extreme diurnal variation.

The modern history of the estate dates from the ownership of Bob Travers, who built up the property from 1968 and made some famous Cabernet Sauvignons in the seventies. But the property became run down in recent years, and by the time it was sold in 2013, most wine came from grapes purchased from growers on Mount Veeder. After some problems between the new partners, the Schottenstein family took 100% ownership in 2016. They are replanting 85% of the vineyards, but believe it will be a fifteen year process before Mayacamas returns completely to estate production. "Bob Travers made a huge variety of wines, but we are confining the focus to Cabernet Sauvignon, Merlot, and Chardonnay," says sales manager Artie Johnson.

The intention is to keep the style of Mayacamas: "We are replanting with heritage clones because we don't want to change the style in the glass." For Chardonnay, this is relatively lean, with minimal exposure to new oak and malolactic fermentation blocked. "The wine tends to start very simple and closed down, and then it begins to develop around the time of release," explains winemaker Braiden Albrecht. It takes another year for flavor variety to develop. Current releases of the Cabernet show increased purity from the old style, with a sense of the precision of the black fruits reinforced by the volcanic mountain soils. While this is very much a work in progress, there is good potential for Mayacamas to define the classic character of mountain Cabernet.

Château Montelena

**

1429 Tubbs Lane, Calistoga, CA 94515

+1 707 942 5105

Jeff Adams

reservations@montelena.com

www.montelena.com

Calistoga

Cabernet Sauvignon, Montelena Estate

Napa Valley, Chardonnay

② Napa Valley, Cabernet Sauvignon

😊 $30 🏭 🚚 🚜

247 acres; 400,000 bottles [map p. 36]

Chateau Montelena is that rare thing in California: a real chateau, originally called the A. L. Tubbs Winery after its founder, who constructed it in 1888. Jim Barrett bought the property and vineyard and revived it from its dilapidated state to start making wine in 1972. Today the wine is made by Jim's son, Bo Barrett.

Although Chateau Montelena won the Judgment of Paris for its Chardonnay, its Cabernet Sauvignon was one of the trendsetters through the 1970s. This has now become the Montelena Estate bottling, sourced from the vineyards around the winery at the very northern limit of Napa Valley. The elevation is around 400 foot, which no doubt compensates for the increase in temperature that's usually found going up the valley. The wine is a blend from several sites that ripen over a 4-6 week period, increasing complexity. It has a long and distinguished reputation for elegance.

But there is also another, completely different, Cabernet Sauvignon, also under the Napa Valley appellation, which comes from other vineyards and is made in a much simpler style. The only distinction between them on the bottle is a gold band stating "The Montelena Estate" on the original bottling. It would be easy to become confused. Personally, I like the older vintages better than the more powerful recent vintages; the 1985 was still going strong in 2012. Neither the white nor red shows New World exuberance; the style is relatively restrained, but there's a tendency in more recent vintages for the wines to tighten up and become leaner, losing that flush of youthful fruit that makes them so attractive.

Morlet Family Vineyards ★★

2825 St. Helena Highway North, St. Helena, CA 94574

+1 707 967 8690

Luc & Jodie Morlet

info@morletwines.com

www.morletwines.com

St. Helena

Sonoma Coast, Joli Coeur Pinot Noir

Napa, Passionément Cabernet Sauvignon

Sonoma County, Ma Douce Chardonnay

$150

69 acres; 72,000 bottles
[map p. 37]

"I don't see myself as a traditionalist, we define our winemaking as neoclassical, neo for the New World and classical because we represent a thousand years of winemaking (in France)," says Luc Morlet. The restored mansion that is Morlet's headquarters is just behind St. Helena, looking out towards the Vaca mountains. The atmosphere feels more residential than commercial. Luc comes from Champagne, and visits start with a glass of champagne from the family domain, Pierre Morlet.

Luc started in Napa by making wine at Newton and Peter Michael, and began producing his own wine in 2006. He has been accumulating vineyards, with a couple of acres around the house, a small parcel in Knights Valley, and most recently an abandoned vineyard on the Oakville Bench. Production will be three quarters based on estate grapes, split more or less equally between Napa and Sonoma, although moving more towards Napa as the estate vineyards come on line. Cabernet Sauvignons come from Napa, while Pinot Noir and Chardonnay come from Sonoma. In each case, there are both cuvées from specific vineyards and blends from different sources. "All the wines are terroir-driven, but as a Champenoise I believe in assemblage. (Chardonnays) Ma Douce and Ma Princesse are exclusively about terroir, but Coup de Coeur is a barrel selection of the best lots." The same approach is followed with other varieties.

Almost all the great French varieties are made here. The varietal Passionément shows the direct purity of Cabernet Sauvignon fruits, the Mon Chevalier blend shows typically more breadth. The Syrah (Bouquet Garni) resembles the Northern Rhône aromatically but shows the fullness of the New World on the palate. The Pinot Noirs are characteristically earthy, sweet, and ripe. Chardonnays are in the New World tradition, full bodied and rich, but with a flavor spectrum that brings Burgundy to mind. There is even a Sémillon-Sauvignon Blanc blend (La Proportion Dorée) intended to resemble Pessac-Léognan. All the wines have French names, and Luc is busy recapitulating the aromas and flavors of his native France, although the wines have the richer, full-bodied quality of the New World.

Newton Vineyard

**

2555 Madrona Avenue, St. Helena, CA 94574

+1 707 963 9000

Robb Mann

@

winery@newtonvineyard.com

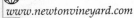
www.newtonvineyard.com

St. Helena

Napa Unfiltered Cabernet Sauvignon

Carneros Chardonnay

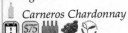

232 acres; 144,000 bottles [map p. 37]

After founding Sterling Vineyards in Calistoga in the 1960s and then selling to Coca Cola in the 1970s, Peter Newton founded the vineyard with his name at St. Helena in 1977. Then in 2001 LVMH purchased a small share, followed by a majority share (90%) in 2006. Rob Mann came from LVMH's Cape Mentelle property in Margaret River, Australia, to become chief winemaker in 2014 to refresh a winemaking style that had become a little tired.

Newton is a beautiful property with terraced vineyards climbing at all angles on to Spring Mountain above St. Helena. Vineyards occupy less than a quarter of the extensive estate, and extend from 500 to 1,600 feet elevation. The estate is planted with Cabernet Sauvignon (90%) and Merlot. There is also a sizeable vineyard on Mount Veeder, and smaller vineyards in Yountville as well as Carneros and Knights Valley. There is one Cabernet Sauvignon (billed as single vineyard) from each of the three major estates; these represent significantly lower yields than the other cuvées. They are sold only directly from the winery. There is a Bordeaux blend (typically with just over half Cabernet Sauvignon), called Puzzle, from Spring Mountain. Chardonnays come from Knights Valley, Carneros, and Mount Veeder. All the wines are unfiltered, but there is a less expensive range called the Unfiltered, simply labeled as Napa Valley, which includes Cabernet Sauvignon, Pinot Noir, and Chardonnay.

The difference between the ranges is nicely indicated by the Chardonnays: the Napa Unfiltered (a blend from Mount Veeder and Carneros) makes something of a full, rich, traditional impression, but Knights Valley and Carneros are less obvious and have more distinctive characters, the former quite restrained with some herbal impressions, and the latter something of a halfway house with a granular texture. The general house style is on the tight side when young. The Cabernets have tannins that are firm but not aggressive; fruits tend to tautness and elegance but take several years to emerge from their youthful tightness. The Yountville is perhaps the most approachable of the single vineyards.

The winery was destroyed by the Glass Fire of 2020.

Nickel & Nickel

*

 8164 St. Helena Highway, Oakville, CA 94562

📞 +1 707 967 9600

📇 Darice Spinelli

@

info@nickelandnickel.com

🌐

www.nickelandnickel.com

🌎 Oakville

 Rutherford, Quarry Cabernet Sauvignon

264,000 bottles

[map p. 36]

Nickel & Nickel displays its origin as a farm with horses in a paddock alongside route 29, and a series of barns behind, which contain tasting rooms, storage facilities, and the winery. The heart of the property is the Sullenger House, originally built in the 1880s, and now used for reception. Together with the surrounding vineyard, the property was purchased by Gil and Beth Nickel, the owners of Nickel & Nickel (just close by) in 1997. A majority stake in both Nickel & Nickel and Far Niente was sold to GI Partners, a San Francisco private equity firm, in 2016.

Nickel & Nickel focuses on a series of 100% varietal single-vineyard wines. Cabernet is the heart, with fifteen different wines representing vineyards in seven of the Napa AVAs. There are also three Merlots from Napa AVAs, a Syrah from Russian River, and three Chardonnays from Carneros and Russian River. Individual vineyards vary from 2-25 acres; sources include estate grapes and long term contracts with growers. "When we say single vineyard, we mean single varietal as well. We do that because we don't want you to see a difference because there's a change in the blend. We want to showcase the vineyard, so we try to reduce the variables, we can't use a lot of the techniques that people use," says winemaker Darice Spinelli.

Defining a house style would be difficult with the range of vineyards; just a sample shows the extent of variety, from stern Hayne vineyard in St. Helena, elegant velvety Quarry vineyard in Rutherford, savory impressions from Copper Streak Vineyard in Stags Leap, and restrained tautness in Sori Bricco from Diamond Mountain. Within Oakville, Rock Cairn Vineyard is finely textured but aromatic, Branding Iron is smoother and softer, and John Sullenger is stern but promises elegance. The single-vineyard wines offer an unusual opportunity to compare different parts of Napa, and even different sites in Oakville or Rutherford, with minimal variation aside from source.

Opus One

***

📍 *7900 St. Helena Highway, Oakville, CA 94562*

📞 *+1 707 944 9442*

👤 *Michael Silacci*

@ *info@opusonewinery.com*

🌐 *www.opusonewinery.com*

📍 *Oakville*

🍷 *Opus One*

2️⃣ *Ouverture*

🎫 $50 🏭 🚚 🚜

168 acres; 300,000 bottles
[map p. 38]

Created as a joint venture between Robert Mondavi and Baron Philippe de Rothschild in 1979, Opus One was one of the first collaborations between Bordeaux and Napa winemakers. Before Opus One had its own vineyards, grapes came from Mondavi's holding of To Kalon, so the first vintage in 1979 was really more of a super-cuvée than Opus One as it later developed. The wine was made at Mondavi until Opus One's winery was constructed in 1991. Across route 29 from Mondavi, the Opus One winery is a somewhat bunker-like building nestled into the hillside.

The first estate vineyard was established when Mondavi sold the 14 ha Q block of the To Kalon vineyard to the new venture. Further vineyards directly across route 29 were purchased in 1983 and 1984, and another 19 ha of To Kalon were added in 2004. Over the years the vineyards have been steadily replanted at higher vine density with lower-yielding clones.

After Constellation Brands acquired Mondavi in 2004, Opus One became completely independent. "The dissolution of the partnership (between the owners of Opus One) was a catalyst for change," says Michael Silacci. "This is more of an independent operation now." A second wine, Ouverture, is available only at the winery, produced from declassified lots; it is intended to be less structured than Opus One and more approachable in its youth. It's not vintage-dated, and production is around 10%.

"The assumption from the beginning was that there should be a Bordeaux blend," says Michael Silacci, but there's always a high content of Cabernet Sauvignon (usually over 85%). Initially the blend started with Cabernet Franc and Merlot; Malbec was added in 1994 and Petit Verdot was added in 1997. The wine is easy to under-rate in the early years, when it tends to be somewhat dumb, with a touch of austerity. The wine shows beautifully after 10 years, and after 20 years shows increased elegance. The very first vintage remains vibrant today.

Pahlmeyer Winery

811 St. Helena Highway, St. Helena, CA94574 (offices)

, 850 Bordeaux Way, Suite #7 Napa, CA 94558 (tasting room)

+1 707 255 2321

info@pahlmeyer.com

www.pahlmeyer.com

St. Helena

Napa Proprietary Red

72 acres; 264,000 bottles [map p. 37]

Pahlmeyer's history recapitulates the flamboyance of the early years in Napa. It started with Jayson Pahlmeyer's intention to make a "California Mouton" at a site in southern Napa. Against advice from the University at Davis that the site was best suited to growing corn, Jayson planted it with Bordeaux varieties, using plant material smuggled in from Bordeaux. The first release of the Proprietary Red was in 1986. Sources have changed; in 199, Pahlmeyer developed the Waters Ranch on Atlas Peak, and today the wine is a blend from Waters Ranch together with grapes sourced from other mountain vineyards, particularly Stagecoach Vineyard on Atlas Peak, and Rancho Chimiles in Wooden Valley. Following Mouton, it is more than 80% Cabernet Sauvignon with small amounts of all the other Bordeaux varieties. There is also a Merlot, sourced from the estate and Stagecoach. A second label, Jayson by Pahlmeyer, was added in 1992.

The style is forceful: even the Merlot is stern and powerful. "We are trying to make another level of California Merlot, planted in cooler spots on the mountain to give it the structure and acidity it needs," says Cleo Pahlmeyer, who took over from her father in 2017. So is the reference point still Bordeaux? "Our benchmark is our own wines, and some from other producers," Cleo says. In addition to the Proprietary Red and Merlot, there is a Napa Chardonnay, and two small barrel selections from the estate, available only to the mailing list. Alcohol levels range from 15-16%. Everything is full-force here; perhaps the best single word to describe the wines is hedonistic.

Gallo purchased the Pahlmeyer Winery and the Jayson by Pahlmeyer range, and leased the Waters Ranch from Pahlmeyer, in 2019. The sale did not include the Wayfarer brand, which Jayson started in Sonoma to make Pinot Noir, and which Cleo Pahlmeyer continues to run (see profile in *Guide to Sonoma*).

Philip Togni Vineyard

*

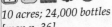

3780 Spring Mountain Rd,
St. Helena, CA 94574

+1 707 963 3731

Lisa Togni

tognivyd@wildblue.net

www.philiptognivineyard.com

St. Helena

Cabernet Sauvignon

Tanbark

10 acres; 24,000 bottles
[map p. 36]

Philip Togni was first involved in planting Cabernet Sauvignon in 1959, and worked in a variety of countries before coming to Cuvaison in Napa. He was involved with several mountain vineyards, including Pride and Chappellet (he made the 1969 Chappellet Cabernet, which is considered one of the great successes of the decade), before he started to clear the land for his own vineyard in 1975, when he planted the first 3 acres of Sauvignon Blanc, followed by 1.5 acres of Cabernet Franc in 1981, all on AxR1. By 1985 everything had been replanted on 110 rootstock.

The estate is at the top of Spring Mountain, close to the border between Napa and Sonoma. It's set well back from the road, and you are given detailed instructions on how to find the unmarked driveway (and to lock the gate behind you). Philip's daughter Lisa is now slowly taking over the winemaking. There are three lines of wines: Togni estate, Tanbark (a second label, introduced pretty much right at the beginning, in 1986), and Ca'Togni (only for sweet wine made from Black Hamburg). "We started off saying we wanted to make a Médoc wine," Philip says, and his Cabernet Sauvignon is typically about 86% Cabernet Sauvignon, with the rest from the other three Bordeaux varieties. Merlot is a little under represented in the wine (6%) compared to plantings (15%) because its yields are lower than the other varieties. The current vintage, together with ten year old wines from a library, is offered to subscribers in the Fall. The wines are intended for the long haul.

Pride Mountain Vineyards ★★

4026 Spring Mountain Road, St. Helena, CA 94574

+1 707 963 4949

Lacey Olsen

@

reservations@pridewines.com

www.pridewines.com

St. Helena

Reserve Claret, Cabernet Sauvignon

$30

84 acres; 200,000 bottles [map p. 36]

Pride is located right at the peak of Spring Mountain. In fact, the vineyards straddle the line between Napa and Sonoma (one inconvenient consequence being that regulations require two bonded wineries, one for handling Napa wines, the other for Sonoma). The origin of every lot has to be tracked. If a wine has more than 75% of grapes from Napa, it can be labeled with the Napa AVA, but most wines carry complicated accounts of the percent coming from Napa County versus Sonoma County.

Vineyards are around 2,000 feet, above the fog line, with 60% on the Sonoma side. Plantings are mostly Bordeaux varieties, with a little Syrah and small amounts of Chardonnay and Viognier. There are three different Cabernet Sauvignons and also a "Claret." The largest production, around 5,000 cases, is the Estate Cabernet Sauvignon, which usually has a bit more fruit from Napa than Sonoma. Winemaker Sally Johnson says this is at its peak for drinking about one year after release, although personally I'd prefer to wait another year.

The two higher tiers are Vintner Select (500-600 cases) and the Reserve Cabernet Sauvignon (1,200 cases). "Vintner Select is the epitome of the California style, flashy and showy, it's 100% Napa," says Sally. It's a 100% Cabernet Sauvignon exclusively from clone 337. The Reserve is a more masculine wine intended for longer aging. "Not many people are making wines like the Reserve," she says. This sometimes has a couple of percent Petit Verdot, and is dominated by Pride's own Rock Arch clone of Cabernet Sauvignon. There's also the Reserve Claret, which is a Merlot-Cabernet Sauvignon blend.

Robert Foley ★★

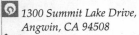

 1300 Summit Lake Drive, Angwin, CA 94508

📞 *+1 707 965 2669*

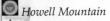 *Bob Foley*

@
info@robertfoleyvineyards.com.

🌐
www.robertfoleyvineyards.com

 Howell Mountain

🕯 *Napa Valley, Cabernet Sauvignon*

120,000 bottles
[map p. 36]

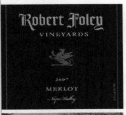

Bob Foley started working for Heitz in the 1970s, moved to Markham, and then to Pride, and altogether has made 35 vintages in Napa. He started Robert Foley in 1998, with a single wine called Claret. He gained access to more vineyards over the following years, planted his own vineyard, and Claret graduated into a 100% Cabernet because they started bottling the Merlot separately. Until 2003 the wine was a blend, from 2004 to 2005 it had 7% Merlot, since 2006 it has been 100% Cabernet Sauvignon. Production was 500 cases when he started, today it is 10,000 altogether, but it's still a small company. There are now 5 acres planted on Howell Mountain, but most of the grapes are purchased. With 2010 he has gone back to a Bordeaux blend for Claret and will have a separate Cabernet bottling. He is fussy about clones: "Clones of Cabernet are very important. I work with three main clones: the two old clones 4 and 7 are my favorites for masculinity. The newest clone I work with (since 1992) is 337 for its femininity," he says.

Robert Mondavi Winery

*

7801 St. Helena Highway, Oak-ville, CA 94562

+1 888 766 6328

@

spotlight@robertmondaviwinery.com

www.robertmondavi.com

Oakville

Napa Valley, Cabernet Sauvignon Reserve

😊 $25 🏭 🍷 🍸 🌱

741 acres; 2,700,000 bottles
[map p. 38]

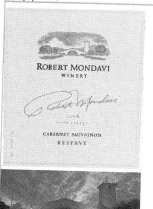

Mondavi scarcely needs any introduction as an icon of Napa Valley. The winery was built in 1966 and the first vintage of Cabernet Sauvignon was released in 1968. The 1974 Reserve Cabernet was one of the wines that put Napa Valley Cabernet on the map. The company broadened out with the introduction in 1979 of the cheaper Woodbridge brand from Lodi. Mondavi continued to be run by the Mondavi family, with Robert's son Tim as winemaker, although it became a publicly quoted company, until it was sold to conglomerate Constellation for $1.36 billion in 2004. (Tim Mondavi now makes wine at his own, company, Continuum: see mini-profile.)

Today Mondavi produces three Cabernet Sauvignons. The Napa Valley bottling is dominated by grapes from To Kalon and Stags Leap District (typically around a third each); Cabernet Sauvignon is 75-85% with Cabernet Franc and Merlot as second in importance. The Oakville bottling is dominated by To Kalon (typically more than three quarters): it has slightly more Cabernet Sauvignon, with Cabernet Franc as the second variety, and small amounts of Merlot, Malbec, and Petit Verdot. The flagship Napa Valley Reserve comes largely (sometimes almost exclusively) from To Kalon. It's usually more than 85% Cabernet Sauvignon; Merlot tended to be the second variety in the early years, but since the mid nineties Cabernet Franc has been second. Petit Verdot made its first appearance in the blend in 1997. In addition, in occasional vintages there is a bottling of a To Kalon Cabernet Sauvignon (from a block of old vines) or a Stags Leap District Cabernet Sauvignon, both 100% varietal. Mondavi also produces Chardonnay, of course, but in some ways is better known for the Fumé Blanc, a Sauvignon Blanc matured in oak barriques; the Reserve To-Kalon bottling has great depth and character, with potential for aging.

Schrader Cellars **

4405 Silverado Trail, Calistoga, CA 94515

☎ +1 707 942 1212

👤 Thomas Brown

@ info@schradercellars.com

🌐 www.schradercellars.com

📍 Calistoga

🍾 CCS, Cabernet Sauvignon

🚫 @ 🛢 🚜

0 acres; 22,000 bottles
[map p. 36]

Fred Schrader cofounded Colgin-Schrader Cellars in 1992, and then moved to found Schrader Cellars with his wife Carol in 1998. There are about six cuvées, all Cabernet Sauvignon, coming from grapes purchased from Andy Beckstoffer's top vineyards. The present portfolio concentrates on single vineyard bottlings from To Kalon and the George III vineyard. The wines are among the highest priced from Napa, usually above $350 per bottle on release.

The To Kalon bottlings emphasize small plots within the vineyard, mostly planted with individual clones. The first year of production from To Kalon was 2000, but 2001 was the year when the Schraders moved to an acreage contract, giving them control over issues such as harvesting, which is late, usually at the start of October. The style has always been towards powerful cult wines, ripe, rich, and full, but the massive underlying structure takes them far away from fruit bombs. They use whole berry fermentation, lasting 12-18 days, the wine goes to barrels of new oak just before the end of fermentation (which gives better integration with the wood), then goes through MLF and spends 14-18 months in the wood, which are barrels from Duamaji made for Merlot on the Right Bank of Bordeaux.

The characters of the individual bottlings demonstrate the relative differences between Cabernet Sauvignon clones at a high level of concentration and ripeness, with clone 6 the most structured, 337 the most opulent, and clone 4 the most loose knit. "Clone 337 doesn't have the steely backbone that 4 and 6 have; the wine is more right-bankish and ready to go," Fred says.

It was a surprise when Schrader sold the brand to giant producer Constellation in 2017 (for $60 million). As there are no vineyards, the purchase basically involves the small inventory and the contracts for purchasing grapes. It is uncertain whether and how the brand may change now.

Screaming Eagle Winery ***

🔾 *Silverado Trail, Oakville, CA 94558*

📞 *+1 707 944 0749*

📇 *Armand de Maigret*

@ *winery@screamingeagle.com*

🌐 *www.screamingeagle.com*

🔵 *Oakville*

🍷 *Screaming Eagle*

② *Second Flight*

🚫 📧 🍇 🍂

44 acres; 13,000 bottles
[map p. 38]

Screaming Eagle scarcely needs any introduction: it is by far California's most famous cult wine. The winery was created when Jean Phillips bought 23 ha of land just off the Silverado trail, in the Oakville area, for an unusually high price in 1986. The area was known to the neighbors as providing high quality grapes; largely Riesling, it was replanted to Cabernet Sauvignon in 1987 with small amounts of Merlot and Cabernet Franc. Heidi Barrett was engaged as winemaker. Since then, further replanting, managed by David Abreu, has brought the vineyard into a Bordeaux-like balance of Cabernet Sauvignon, Cabernet Franc, and Merlot.

The slight depression in the land creates a small frost problem from time to time, which is handled by overhead sprinklers fed by a lake. Drainage has been installed under the new plantings to recapture water. They expect to dry farm more or less around two thirds of the ranch, especially where there's more clay (to the west). This is an early ripening site, but even so, they are early pickers here, usually a week to ten days ahead of everyone else. The Cabernet has historically been clones 7 and See, but in the last couple of years some clones 6, 169, and 337 have crept in.

The winery was sold in 2006 to two partners, one of whom has since left. Stanley Kroenke, who made his fortune in agriculture, is now the sole owner. Armand de Maigret manages Screaming Eagle and Kroenke's other wine properties, which include Jonata and The Hilt, in Californian coastal regions, and most recently, Bonneau du Martray in Corton Charlemagne.

Shafer Vineyards

**

 6154 Silverado Trail,
Napa, CA 94558

📞 +1 707 944 2877

☎ John Gretz

@

info@shafervineyards.com

🌐

www.shafervineyards.com

 Stags Leap District

🏔 Stags Leap District, Cabernet Sauvignon

205 acres; 384,000 bottles
[map p. 39]

John Shafer left a career in corporate publishing to move to Napa Valley, where he purchased 210 acres and planted vineyards in 1972 in what became the Stags Leap District in 1989. The first vintage in 1978 used Cabernet Sauvignon from the Sunspot vineyard that rises up immediately above the winery. Hillside Select started in 1983, when Doug Shafer became winemaker. "I was tasting lots and the Sunspot was head and shoulders above everything else. I thought we should bottle it separately—this became the 1982 Reserve. That started the program. I got tired of explaining what Reserve was, because everyone had a reserve, and in 1983 we called it Hillside Select. The fruits are so good you can keep your hands off it—Hillside Select is the easiest wine to make," Doug says.

There are about 20 ha on the hillside block, and the best lots are selected each year for Hillside Select, of which there are usually 2,000-2,500 cases. It's 100% Cabernet Sauvignon. There are also about 8,000 cases of the One Point Five Cabernet Sauvignon, which comes from the hillside estate vineyard and the Borderline vineyard two miles south of Shafer at the edge of the Stags Leap District. Other wines include Chardonnay, Merlot, and Syrah. The style is rich and lush, distinctly New World, for all the wines, although Hillside Select seems to have toned down a little with recent vintages.

Robert Sinskey Vineyards

*

6320 Silverado Trail, Napa, CA 94558

+1 707 944 9090

Conner Burns or Phil Abram

rsv@robertsinskey.com

www.robertsinskey.com

Stags Leap District

Carneros, Four Vineyards, Pinot Noir

😊 $40 👑 🍇 🍂

200 acres; 275,000 bottles [map p. 39]

The modern winery is located on the Silverado Trail in Napa Valley, but the vineyards are in Carneros, where Sinskey has four Pinot Noir vineyards (there is also a vineyard in Sonoma). About half of all production is Pinot Noir, making Sinskey a Pinot Noir specialist in the area. Wines are made only from estate fruit. At one point the vineyards were all heirloom selections, but after phylloxera they were replanted with Dijon and Pommard. Rob is now looking for more heirloom selections. "Dijon clones produce ripe fruit and lower acid, usually showy, but missing what I go to Pinot Noir for."

Until 2001 Sinskey made a Carneros Pinot Noir and a reserve bottling, but felt that "Reserve" had little meaning since the wines were not produced in a rich oaky style, so the change was made to single vineyard bottlings. Rob sees the winery as a bridge between old and new worlds. "Russian River is the competition in the markets, but stylistically the competition is Burgundy or Oregon." The vineyards have different characters, and harvest dates for Pinot are spread over about four weeks. There is complete destemming for all wines, cap irrigation during fermentation rather than punch-down to give better control of extraction, and maturation in 30% new oak. The wines are intended to drink well from soon after the vintage, and Rob says that he sees about ten years as the natural life span for most vintages.

Carneros is the entry-level Pinot, made in a more forward style than is intended to drink sooner. Four Vineyards is a blend from each of Sinskey's individual Pinot Noir vineyards: it's more elegant than the Carneros blend, but has less personality than the single-vineyard wines. Vandal vineyard, on the hillside of Northern Carneros close to the town of Napa, is the first to pick and the leanest. "Its characteristic note is the bright fruit with a cranberry essence," Rob says. The Three Amigos vineyard is right off the San Pablo Bay, just by the Napa marina; usually the last to be harvested, it's more rounded and less acid. Capa is a small vineyard in the sunniest location; planted mostly with Dijon clones, it is usually the most "Californian" in style of Sinskey's Pinot Noirs, with more black than red fruits.

Spottswoode Estate Vineyard & Winery   *

*1902 Madrona Avenue,
St. Helena, CA 94574*

+1 707 963 0134

Beth Novak Milliken

@

estate@spottswoode.com

www.spottswoode.com

St. Helena

*St. Helena, Cabernet
Sauvignon*

Lyndenhurst

$75

*40 acres; 84,000 bottles
[map p. 37]*

Driving along Madrona Avenue in downtown St. Helena through suburban housing, you wonder where the Spottswoode winery can be, and then suddenly you come out into 15 hectares of vineyards that stretch from the edge of the town up to the mountains. Jack and Mary Novak purchased the property in 1972, and were refused a permit to make wine because the neighborhood was residential. The later purchase (in 1990) of a winery across the road allowed the wine to be made in the vicinity.

The Cabernet Sauvignon is a blend, although there is no Merlot. "We don't have any Merlot growing here, I'm not a fan of Merlot in this area. There was some Merlot at Spottswoode long ago, but it was removed," says winemaker Aron Weinkauf. In addition to 12.5 ha of Cabernet Sauvignon, there are 1.25 ha of Cabernet Franc and 0.4 ha of Petit Verdot for the blend, and also a hectare of Sauvignon Blanc. A second wine, called Lyndenhurst, is made in a more approachable fruit-forward, less ageworthy style (using 60% new oak compared to Spottswoode's 68%). Production is usually about 3,000 cases of Spottswoode and 700 cases of Lyndenhurst. My favorite vintage of Spottswoode is the 1992.

Stag's Leap Wine Cellars

5766 Silverado Trail, Napa CA 94558

+1 707 944 2020

Marcus Notaro

retail@cask23.com

www.cask23.com

Stags Leap District

Fay Vineyard, Cabernet Sauvignon

240 acres; 1,800,000 bottles [map p. 39]

Stag's Leap Wine Cellars has a special place in the history of Napa for gaining first place for its 1973 Cabernet in the Judgment of Paris tasting in Paris in 1976. Coming ahead of three first growth Bordeaux from the 1970 vintage, this stamped Napa Valley Cabernet as a serious contender on the world stage. Stag's Leap had been started by Warren Winiarski only just previously, when he purchased a 44 acre plot that he planted as a vineyard in 1970, now known as the SLV (Stag's Leap Vineyard). So 1973 was his first vintage.

Subsequently two wines from Stag's Leap became established as leaders: Cask 23 and Fay's Vineyard. In fact, the original plot had been purchased on the basis of Warren's tasting of wines that had been made from the adjacent Fay vineyard, which Stag's Leap later purchased (in 1986). Cask 23 is based on a election of the best lots from SLV (60%) and Fay's Vineyard (40%); and single-vineyard wines are made from both SLV and Fay's. Fay's vineyard tends to have a softer, more perfumed elegance, while SLV is a bigger wine, with more exotic fruit notes.

In 1996 the vineyard holdings were much expanded by purchasing the 128 acre Arcadia vineyard farther north in Napa Valley. Today a new visitor center has been built in the vineyards. In addition to the top level wines, there's also a mid-level range under the name of Napa Valley Collection and a line or cheaper wines under the Hawk Crest label. In 2007, the winery was sold to a partnership of Chateau Ste. Michelle and Antinori, and since then has somewhat lost its luster. Recent vintages of SLV have been awfully soft for a wine with such a distinguished history. "Too oaky, too fruity, too soft: the very model of a modern Napa Cabernet," my tasting notes say for the most recent vintage. Perhaps the recent arrival of Marcus Notaro from Col Solare (another Ste. Michelle property) will change things.

Staglin Family Vineyard

*1570 Bella Oaks Ln, Ruth-
erford, CA 94573*

+1 707 944 0477

Lindsay Dale

info@staglinfamily.com

www.staglinfamily.com

Rutherford

*Rutherford Cabernet
Sauvignon*

Napa, Salus Chardonnay

Salus

*44 acres; 96,000 bottles
[map p. 38]*

Staglin is one of the wave of wineries founded in the 1980s by people who had been successful elsewhere and decided they wanted to make wine. The old estate had gone through many owners, turned to producing prunes during Prohibition, and then later became part of Beaulieu (contributing to the Georges de Latour Private Reserve), until the Staglins purchased it in 1985. It is right under the Mayacamas Mountains; indeed, the winery, finished in 2002, is a series of tunnels hollowed out into the mountain. The visitor center is in a historic house that was on the property and has been restored.

The estate is 60 acres, but also makes wine from other sources. After the Bella Oaks Vineyard (formerly the basis for a Cabernet Sauvignon from Heitz) was sold to the Booth family in 2010, the Staglins started to produce the Booth Bella Oaks cuvée. In 2015 they shared a purchase of the adjacent Fahrig Ranch, which is planted with Cabernet Sauvignon. David Abreu manages the vineyards; Michel Rolland consults on winemaking. The focus is Cabernet Sauvignon and Chardonnay, with top wines labeled simply as Staglin Family Estate. Salus is a second label, introduced in 1995 (with profits going to a foundation for schizophrenia research), but the Staglins do not regard it as a second wine. "The difference is stylistic: based on selection of barrels that are softer and more straightforward, Salus is intended to be more approachable. Staglin is more complex and structural."

Salus is a smaller production than Staglin itself. The Cabernet Sauvignons usually include very small amounts of other Bordeaux varieties, but the general impression for both labels is full-force varietal, in a rich extracted style. The wine ages relatively quickly, beginning to show tertiary notes after about five years: the Staglins see the sweet spot for the estate Cabernet as ten years after release. The Chardonnay has been similarly intense, with phenolics on the finish, but "We are moving away from what people think of as the California style—buttery and rich—towards more of a fresh fruit style for the Chardonnay." It includes grapes from the Hudson and Hyde vineyards in Carneros. The general house style is rich and oxidative, although for both Chardonnay and Cabernet, Staglin is more muted compared to Salus by a sense of structure in the background.

Trefethen Vineyards

*

1160 Oak Knoll Avenue, Napa, CA 94558

+1 707 255 7700

Janet Trefethen

winery@trefethen.com

www.trefethen.com

Oak Knoll

Oak Knoll Cabernet Sauvignon

Oak Knoll Chardonnay

440 acres; 720,000 bottles
[map p. 39]

When Gene and Katie Trefethen purchased the estate in 1968 it was essentially derelict, and everything had to be restored. Gene had just retired from builder Kaiser Industries, and he intended to grow grapes. That's still reflected in a quarter of the grapes being sold off. However, the next generation, John and Janet Trefethen, prompted the move into winemaking, with the first vintage in 1973. The third generation, Loren and Hailey, is now involved. The main estate is just off route 29; there is a smaller estate in the foothills of the Mayacamas. The original winery was built in 1866; it was damaged in the earthquake of 2014 and is being restored to provide a storage facility. Wine is made in the new winery, built in the 1980s.

When UC Davis was asked for advice when the estate was bought, the answer was "Just plant everything and see what works." That is still reflected in an unusually wide range of wines, with twenty cuvées including Merlots, Cabernets, Malbec, Chardonnays, and Rieslings. "There are not many places in Napa where you can have the diversity of grapes we grow here in Oak Knoll," says winemaker Brian Kays. "We farm the whites for freshness, for reds it is almost the opposite because we are in a cool spot." Asked what is the most typical wine, Brian says, "It would be between the Merlot and the Cabernet but probably the Cabernet; this has a number of things important to Trefethen, it gives the preponderance of fruit but also herbal and spice impressions. And you can taste Oak Knoll in all these wines, by which I mean that you can see the freshness and brightness of acidity."

Few of the wines are monovarietals: the Cabernet usually contains some of Malbec and Petit Verdot, the Merlot usually has some Malbec and Cabernet. Oak is based on French but includes some American and Hungarian, with 40-50% new. Dragon's Tooth is a proprietary red based on Malbec with a lot of Petit Verdot, and is the most aromatic of the red cuvées. The Malbec is a monovarietal expressing the sleek character of the variety. Among whites, the Estate Chardonnay is the most representative as it is a blend from across the whole estate, while Harmony comes from a specific plot and offers a less obvious but richer impression. Both show cool climate character. There are two Rieslings—"We are the largest producer of Riesling in Napa," Brian says—a (relatively) dry Riesling and a late harvest (made by committing a small plot of the vineyard to wait for botrytis). It's hard to define house style across such a wide range, but it's fair to say it achieves the aim of representing the (relatively) fresher character of Oak Knoll.

Turnbull Wine Cellars   *

🔍 *8210 St. Helena Highway, CA 94562*

📞 *+1 800 887 6285*

📇 *Peter Heitz*

@ *reservations@turnbullwines.com*

🌐 *www.turnbullwines.com*

◉ *Oakville*

🍷 *Oakville, Fortuna Cabernet Sauvignon*

😊 🏭 🍇 ☸

165 acres; 192,000 bottles
[map p. 38]

William Turnbull was an architect in San Francisco who bought the first vineyard in the 1970s, when there was just a farmhouse on the property. In 1993 Patrick O'Dell bought the property; his daughter Zoe Johns is now the owner and general manager. The original winery right on route 29 has now become the tasting room, and the present winery (a somewhat practical building) runs back from it. Turnbull has four vineyards: the small home estate surrounds the winery, to the east beyond the Silverado Trail there are the Fortuna Vineyard and Leopoldina (at 1,000 foot elevation). There is also a vineyard in Calistoga.

The focus is on red wine, mostly Cabernet Sauvignon; the only white is Sauvignon Blanc. Only two wines are in general distribution: a Sauvignon Blanc and the Napa Valley Cabernet. The premium wines, coming from individual vineyards, are available only from the winery or through the wine club. There are individual Cabernets from each vineyard and three separate cuvées from plots within Leopoldina. The flagship wine is the Black Label Cabernet, which is a barrel selection of the most powerful lots from all the vineyards, "structured around the heart of darkness," says winemaker Peter Heitz. Nominally the Cabernets are blends, but Cabernet Sauvignon is rarely less than 96%. "In big vintages I might add some Cabernet Franc or Merlot, in vintages needing more oomph I would use Petit Verdot or Malbec," Peter says. New oak is around 50% for the single-vineyard wines. "The vineyards have a big influence, style is more a matter of source than due to the house."

The wines tend to be faintly aromatic, in the direction of violets, forceful but not overwhelming, certainly taut, giving a tight impression when young. Fortuna is the most feminine and shows best when young; Leopoldina is more backward and brooding. Black Label has a sheen of refinement over and above the single-vineyard wines. Peter does not take a position on whether the wines should be drinkable immediately or it should be necessary to wait, but for my palate the power of Oakville is evident and most wines need three or four years after release.

Viader Vineyards

1120 Deer Park Road,
Deer Park, CA 94576

+1 707 963 3816

Delia Viader

tastings@viader.com

www.viader.com

Howell Mountain

Proprietary Red

$75

30 acres; 60,000 bottles
[map p. 36]

Viader Vineyards occupies a steep slope on Howell Mountain that runs down into Bell Canyon. It's at an elevation of 1,200 feet, just below the Howell Mountain AVA. Purchased and then cleared in 1981, the land was planted with Cabernet Sauvignon, Cabernet Franc, and Petit Verdot. There's no Merlot or Malbec because they do not do well in the mountain environment. "I planted Petit Verdot thinking it would go into the Proprietary Red but it just didn't fit," says Delia Viader, explaining why Viader's blend is solely Cabernet Sauvignon and Cabernet Franc. "Differences between the wines are more vintage driven than by variety per se because I change the blend with the vintage," she says.

Cabernet Sauvignon is always a majority, varying from 51-75% over the past decade. The Petit Verdot goes into a monovarietal wine, as does any Cabernet Franc that isn't used for the Proprietary Red; there's also a blended wine that is largely Cabernet Sauvignon and Syrah. Other wines are made from purchased fruit. A change in style may occur as Alex Viader takes over, as he prefers more intensity and extraction. The 2012 shows more power and intensity than previously, but retains that characteristic chocolaty smoothness coming from the Cabernet Franc, and making Viader a distinctive wine.

Vineyard 29

⌖ 2929 Highway 29 North, St. Helena, CA 94574

☎ +1 707 963 9292

👤 Austin Gallion

@ info@vineyard29.com

🌐 www.vineyard29.com

📍 St. Helena

🍷 Napa, 29 Estate Cabernet Sauvignon

📅 $135 🏭 🍇 🛢 🚜

30 acres; 100,000 bottles
[map p. 37]

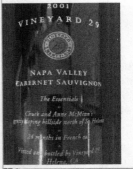

The question driving Vineyard 29 since Chuck and Anne McMinn purchased the property in 2000 has been, "What's the maximum amount of wine I can make and stay at 95 points?" Wine production started at the small vineyard surrounding the winery when the previous owners were persuaded by their neighbors to plant some vines. Success overwhelmed them, and the property became the base for a full commercial operation with the change of ownership in 2000.

The striking post-modern winery was built in 2003 on the elevated site just north of St. Helena with views across to the Vaca Mountains on the other side of the valley. The cave goes back into the mountain behind. There is a tasting room in downtown Napa. The original 2.5 acres at the winery were expanded to 24 acres, and Aida vineyard two miles to the north, previously planted to Zinfandel, was added and mostly replanted to Cabernet.

The winery's capacity of 12,000 cases is split between two ranges. The Vineyard 29 wines are exclusively estate production; there are six different wines, ranging from 50-700 cases per year. The Cru range comes from purchased grapes, including a Napa Cabernet Sauvignon sourced from a variety of vineyards, a Sauvignon Blanc, and a Willamette Pinot Noir. Vineyard 29 wines are sold almost entirely directly by the winery, but Cru is in general distribution (the Cabernet goes mostly to restaurants).

The home estate produces three varietal wines: Cabernet Sauvignon, Cabernet Franc, and Sauvignon Blanc. The Aida vineyard produces Cabernet Sauvignon, Zinfandel (from 45 year-old vines), and a Late Harvest Zinfandel. House style is refined and elegant with a very fine texture, showing quite sweet impressions with lifted aromatics at the end, so the tannins fade into the background. The house style carries through the varieties, with Zinfandel showing more aromatics but not overwhelming (perhaps aided by 15% of Cabernet Sauvignon and Petit Syrah), Cabernet Sauvignon tending to blackcurrants, and Cabernet Franc showing more muted fruits. Austin Gallion at Vineyard 29 says that, "Usually Aida is more muscular and the Estate 29 wines are more refined, but it can vary with the vintage." The 2013 vintage proved so powerful that is being released after the 2014.

ZD Wines   *

[map p. 38]

8383 Silverado Trail,
Napa, CA 94558

+1 707 963 5188

Chris Musante or Barbie Jamieson

info@zdwines.com

www.zdwines.com

Rutherford

Carneros Pinot Noir

$40

37 acres; 360,000 bottles

Brett DeLeuze's father came from aerospace to start the winery with partner Gino Zepponi in 1969, but became sole owner when Gino died in 1985. Members of the DeLeuze family are involved at all levels from winemaking to marketing. The estate started with a 34 acre property in Carneros, where wine was made at weekends; the small property on the Silverado Trail in Rutherford was purchased in 1978; and the winery was built in 1993. A new tasting room was opened in 2018.

ZD makes wine from three varieties: Pinot Noir, Chardonnay, and Cabernet Sauvignon. "With each we make what we consider to be our traditional white label and a reserve wine," Brett says. Typically the white label is based on purchased grapes, and the Reserve comes from the estate.

The white label Chardonnay comes from very varied sources. "We've gone in the opposite direction from most people in making a blend of Chardonnay from four regions, Napa, Carneros-Sonoma, Monterey, and Santa Maria Valley," Brett explains. "We believe the blend is more complex than any one region would be." It showcases rich, tropical fruits, emphasized by fermentation at very low temperature. The Chardonnay Reserve comes from the estate in Carneros and is less forceful. The Pinot Noirs come from Carneros, showing aromatics of earthy strawberries, but Founders Reserve is less overt.

There are three Cabernet Sauvignons: the white label Napa includes a little Petit Verdot; the Founders Reserve is exclusively Cabernet, and Abacus is unusually based on a solera system. The rationale is that the DeLeuze's feel that the increasing complexity of old Cabernet is accompanied by too much loss of fruit. So Abacus is a blend that includes Cabernet Sauvignon from every vintage, kept in old oak barrels. Every year the latest three vintages are added to it to increase volume by 20% and then 15% is drawn off for the current bottling: 2015 is the 18th release. The white label Cabernet is straightforward, the Reserve shows more structure. and Abacus shows much increased refinement. The general house style is sweet and ripe with strong aromatics, reinforced by extensive use of American oak. "We want flavorful delicious wines," is how Brett describes the style.

Mini-Profiles of Important Estates

Accendo Cellars

Wheeler Farms, 588 Zinfandel Lane, St. Helena, CA 94574

+1 707 963 1989

Bart & Daphne Araujo

visits@accendocellars.com

accendocellars.com

St. Helena AVA

12 acres; 16,000 bottles

[map p. 37]

After Bart and Daphne Araujo purchased the Eisele vineyard in 1991, they produced Cabernet Sauvignon (and other varieties) under the name of Araujo Estate. They sold the estate to François Pinault of Château Latour in 2013, and its name was later changed to Eisele Vineyard Estate (see profile). The Araujos started a new venture, which they called Accendo Cellars, based on sourcing grapes from top sources to supplement production from plots in St. Helena and Oak Knoll. They created a custom crush facility at Wheeler Farms in St. Helena, and the wine is made there. The same team is involved as at the old Araujo Estate, including the next Araujo generation, Jaime and Greg, and Michel Rolland as consultant. The focus is on the same varieties: production is split more or less equally between Cabernet Sauvignon and Sauvignon Blanc. The objective remains to make wine in a Bordelais style.

Acumen

1315 First Street, Napa CA 94558 (tasting room)

3265 Soda Canyon Road, Napa CA 94558 (winery)

+1 707 251 8885

Eric Yuan

diana@acumenwine.com

www.acumenwine.com

Atlas Peak AVA

116 acres; 30,000 bottles [map p. 39]

Billionaire Eric Yuang founded Zoom in 2011 and only a year after started his wine project. With the objective of making wine in a more restrained style, he purchased the 32-acre Attelas vineyard at 1,300 foot altitude on Atlas Mountain in 2012 from Dr. Jan Krupp, who had planted it in 1992, three years before he planted Stagecoach Vineyard nearby. A year later, Acumen acquired the 84-acre Edcora vineyard, at 1,600 feet altitude about half a mile away. Plantings are mostly Bordeaux varieties. Phillip Titus is the consulting winemaker. Acumen sells most of its grapes, and makes wine from a selection of small blocks. The Mountainside wines are blends from both sites. The white is Sauvignon Blanc. The red blend has varied from 70-42% Cabernet Sauvignon, with Malbec, Merlot, and Cabernet Franc , and a relatively low (for Napa) alcohol level around 14%. The PEAK range comes from selections of the best plots, with Cabernet Sauvignon (blended from both vineyards), and cuvées from the individual vineyards.

Anderson's Conn Valley Vineyards

680 Rossi Road, St. Helena, CA 94574

+1 707 963 8600

Todd Anderson

cvvinfo@connvalleyvineyards.com

connvalleyvineyards.com

St. Helena AVA

40 acres; 96,000 bottles

[map p. 36]

Gus Anderson was an orthodontist in Michigan before he moved to California. In 1981, he started a new career by purchasing land in Conn Valley, just south of Howell Mountain. He began by planting vines and selling grapes, and then together with his son Todd established a winery. The first vintage was 1987. Gus handed over to Todd in 2001, although he then started a new project, Eagle Trace Winery, which he ran until 2015. The focus is on high-end Cabernet blends: Eloge usually has about 50% Cabernet Sauvignon, while Right Bank has a majority of Cabernet Franc. The flagship wine is the Estate Reserve, almost pure Cabernet Sauvignon. At one extreme there are also some micro-cuvées; at the other, in 2015 a second wine was introduced, just labeled Napa Valley Cabernet Sauvignon. There are also Pinot Noir, Chardonnay, and a white Bordeaux blend.

Antica Napa Valley

3700 Soda Canyon Road, Napa, CA 94558

+1 707 265 8866

info@anticanapavalley.com

anticanapavalley.com

Atlas Peak AVA

600 acres; 60,000 bottles

[map p. 39]

This may be the largest vineyard estate in the mountains around Napa, forming an amphitheater at 1,500-1,800 feet elevation. It started as a joint venture in 1985, called Atlas Peak Vineyard, between Whitbread (the English brewer) and Bollinger Champagme, with Antinori holding a 5% share. The elevation and sight line to San Pablo Bay make the climate unusually moderate for the area. The original vineyard was 120 acres and an attempt to produce Sangiovese, even with Antinori's expertise, was not very successful. "There are lots of similarities [between Atlas Peak and Tuscany]," Piero Antinori said, "but the practical result was the wines were not very interesting." Whitbread and Bollinger sold their share, which ended up with Allied Domecq, who leased the property out. Antinori bought the property in 1993, but the lease still had another decade to run. In the meantime, Antinori bought an adjacent 40-acre vineyard and started to produce wine. The first vintage of the whole property, renamed Antica, was the 2004, released in 2007. (In 2007, Antinori also bought Stag's Leap Wine Cellars.) There is still a Sangiovese, but most of the releases are conventional: Chardonnay, Pinot Noir, Merlot, and Cabernet Sauvignon. The top wine is the single-parcel Townsend Cabernet Sauvignon, named for a (teetotal) neighbor who sold 24 acres of land to Antica. There is also a sweet Muscat and, of course, olive oil.

Arietta

Chateau Boswell, 3468 Silverado Trail, Napa, CA 94574

+1 707 963 5918

Fritz Hatton

info@ariettawine.com

www.ariettawine.com

Oakville AVA

27 acres; 35,000 bottles

[map p. 36]

Arietta started as not so much a winery, more a concept. Meaning a little aria, and in particular the name of a movement from Beethoven's last piano sonata, the name came from a shared interest in music between wine auctioneer Fritz Hatton and John Kongsgaard of Kongsgaard winery (see profile). They started a collaboration in 1996 based on a blend of Cabernet Franc and Merlot from the Hudson Ranch in Carneros. They then added varietal Merlot and the Variation One Merlot-Syrah blend, both also from Hudson Ranch. Production took a new course in 2003 with a Cabernet Sauvignon from one of grower David Abreu's blocks on Howell Mountain. In 2006 the source of the Cabernet shifted to a small block in Coombsville. The best known cuvée is Quartet, introduced in 2004 as a blend of four Bordeaux varieties, based on Cabernet Sauvignon from an Abreu plot in Coombsville; this started out as second wine, but after 2007 shifted to Arietta's equivalent of an entry-level wine in its own right, using sources at the southern end of Napa Valley. In 2005, John Kongsgaard sold his share back to Fritz, and Andy Erickson took over as winemaker, after which some white blends were added. Production is small: Quartet is the largest production run at about 12,000 bottles, and the others can be as low as a few hundred bottles. Although sources focus on (relatively) cool climate vineyards, the style is rich, with lots of new oak used in aging (50% for Quartet is the lowest). The wines were made at Chateau Boswell, on Silverado Trail between St. Helena and Calistoga, but Boswell burned down in the Glass Fire of 2020.

B cellars

703 Oakville Cross Road, Oakville, CA 94562

+1 707 709 8787

concierge@bcellars.com

www.bcellars.com

Oakville AVA

 $70

60,000 bottles

[map p. 36]

Jim Borsack and Duffy Keys were businessmen when they met in 2002. A year later they abandoned their former careers and started B cellars. Grapes come from a variety of sources in Napa—18 different vineyards at last count—and initially wines were made in custom crush facilities. Kirk Venge has been the winemaker from the start. The B cellars winery in Oakville was opened in 2014. Tastings take place in the so-called Hospitality House. In addition to five Beckstoffer cuvées (all Cabernet Sauvignon except for Dr. Crane Cabernet Franc), there are five 100% Cabernet Sauvignons from different sites. There are also some Proprietary Blends, including some unexpected combinations, and Sauvignon Blanc and Chardonnay. Most cuvées are produced in less than 200 cases.

Bacio Divino Cellars

703 Oakville Cross Road, Rutherford, CA 94573

+1 707 942 8101

Claus & Diane Janzen

cloudy@baciodivino.com

www.baciodivino.com

Rutherford AVA

10 acres; 60,000 bottles

[map p. 38]

Prodded by an interest in wine, Claus Janzen moved from Canada to Napa Valley to work at Caymus, eventually becoming the export manager. He made his first wine as a side project in 1993 and then started his own winery, at first making the wine himself, later handing over to Kirk Venge. Grapes come from some plots owned on hillsides east of the Silverado Trail, and also from various Beckstoffer vineyards. Varieties are a little unusual. The original cuvée produced in 1993 was a blend of Sangiovese and Cabernet Sauvignon, and the Bacio Divino estate label now also includes some Petite Syrah. Pazzo, an entry-level wine intended for immediate consumption, is a blend of Sangiovese with Cabernet Sauvignon, Petite Syrah, Syrah, and Viognier. More conventionally, the Cabernet Sauvignon comes from the estate plots plus grapes sourced from Beckstoffer, and there are single-vineyard designates from various Beckstoffer plots, including To-Kalon. The Lucie Pinot Noir comes from grapes sourced in Sonoma. Tastings are held at the Auburn James winery on the Silverado Trail near St. Helena.

Behrens Family Winery

4078 Spring Mountain Road, St. Helena, CA 94574

+1 917 842 0976

Les & Lisa Behrens

robin@behrensfamilywinery.com

www.behrensfamilywinery.com

Spring Mountain District AVA

 $65

0 acres; 54,000 bottles

[map p. 36]

Starting as a collaboration between the Behrens and Hitchcock families, the original name was the Behrens and Hitchcock winery. The Hitchcocks retired in 2005, and Les and Lisa Behrens changed the name to Behrens Family Winery. Les has been the winemaker since 1993, when the wine was made at the Behrens home in Arcata, California, where the Behrens had a restaurant. Production moved to a winery constructed on top of Spring Mountain in 1999, but grapes are sourced from plots all over Napa Valley. Most wines are varietals made in small quantities; cuvées may change from year to year. Les and Lisa describe their style as "rich and powerful." Tastings used to be held in a trailer at the winery, and then moved to a tasting room in St. Helena before a new tasting room was constructed at the winery. The winery burned down in the Glass Fire of 2020.

Bennett Lane Winery

3340 Highway 128, Calistoga, CA 94515
+1 707 942 6684
Stefanie Longton
info@bennettlane.com
www.bennettlane.com
Calistoga AVA

🚶 💲20 🏭 🍇 🍾 🍷

22 acres; 132,000 bottles

About the most northern winery in Napa Valley, just beyond Tubbs Lane, Bennett Lane was created as Vigil Vineyards in 1898, and came under the ownership of Randy and Lisa Lynch in 2003. The 7 acre home vineyard is just north of the winery, and there are another 15 ha close by on the valley floor. Grapes are also sourced from other sites in the valley. The entry-level wines are the Maximus white (a blend of Sauvignon Blanc, Chardonnay, and a little Muscat) and red (71% Cabernet Sauvignon, 12% Syrah, 12% Merlot, and 5% Malbec). The Reserve Chardonnay comes from Carneros and has 30% malolactic fermentation. Moving into Cabernet Sauvignon, there is a Napa release, the Reserve almost doubles the price, and the top wine is the Lynch Family Calistoga AVA. All age in barriques with 30% new oak. The Tubbs Fire destroyed the 2017 vintage, but the vineyards recovered next year.

Blackbird Vineyards

1330 Oak Knoll Ave, Napa, CA 94558
+1 707 252 4444
John Hinshaw
info@blackbirdvineyards.com
www.blackbirdvineyards.com
Oak Knoll AVA

📱 🏭 🍇 🍾 🍷

25 acres; 30,000 bottles [map p. 39]

The home vineyard was owned by Trefethen and sold fruit to several wineries before it was purchased by investment banker Michael Polenske in 2003 to create Blackbird Vineyards (which is part of a general holding called Bespoke Collections). John and Julia Hinshaw, who were investors in Blackbird, purchased a majority interest in 2019. Located in Oak Knoll, the vineyard was entirely planted to Merlot in 1997. Grapes are also sourced from other vineyards all over the valley. Aaron Pott is the winemaker. The range starts with the Arriviste rosé, based on a Bordeaux blend, and the Dissonance Sauvignon Blanc (which contains 10-15% Sémillon). The focus on reds is towards blends based on Right Bank varieties, In Bordeaux-style, there is significant variation in the blend from year to year. Merlot is the predominant variety in Arise (37-75%) and Illustration (48-81%); Cabernet Franc is the predominant variety (41-82%) in Paramour; and Contrarian has variously had a majority of Cabernet Sauvignon, Cabernet Franc, or Merlot. The Blackmail series of 100% varietals is available only to members of the mailing list.

BOND Estates

P.O. Box 426, Oakville, CA 94562
+1 707 944 9445
Summer Jimenez
info@bond.wine
www.bond.wine
Oakville AVA

🚫 @ 🍇 🚜

0 acres; 24,000 bottles

Bill Harlan is best known for his ambition of producing a 'first growth' wine at Harlan Estate (see profile). BOND started as a separate project in 1997, with same winemaking team headed by Bob Levy. The objective is to express Cabernet Sauvignon in different terroirs. Grapes are sourced from individual vineyards ranging from 7 to 11 acres in a variety of locations on both sides of the valley. BOND does not own the vineyards, but manages them. It can take several years before the grapes are used for a BOND cuvée. At last count there were five cuvées. Melbury is opposite Pritchard Hill, near Lake Hennessy, Quella is in Spring Valley near Joseph Phelps, St. Eden is on an alluvial fan on the west of Lake Prichard, Vecina is just southwest of Oakville AVA on the edge of the Mayacamas Mountains, and Pluribus is on Spring Mountain. I find the style of the BOND cuvées to be noticeably richer and more obviously New World in origin than that of Harlan.

Burgess Cellars

1108 Deer Park Road, St. Helena,
CA 94574

+1 800 752 9463

Steven Burgess

vino@burgesscellars.com

www.burgesscellars.com

St. Helena AVA

62 acres; 200,000 bottles
[map p. 37]

Located at 1,000 foot altitude on Howell Mountain, although not in the AVA, Burgess Cellars was one of the first wineries established when Napa Valley got going. (Previously the property was the base for Souverain winery, now located in Sonoma.) The winery built in the 1880s was destroyed in the Glass Fire of 2020. Tom Burgess was a former air force pilot who founded the winery in 1972; his sons Steven and James are in charge today The 1880 Estate Vineyard consists of 30 acres on volcanic soil facing west around the winery; higher up, with more sedimentary soils facing east at 1,200 foot elevation, the 31 acre Haymaker Vineyard was added in 1978. At one time Burgess also owned a vineyard in Oak Knoll, but that was sold to Heitz, so the sole focus now is on mountain grapes. Bill Sorenson was the winemaker from 1972 to 2012, and focused on Cabernet Sauvignon. The lead wine is the Hillside Vineyards Cabernet Sauvignon; at about twice the price, the Reserve Cabernet Sauvignon is a blend of 85% Cabernet Sauvignon, 10% Petit Verdot, 2.5% Malbec, and 2.5% Merlot. Kelly Woods became the winemaker in 2013 and introduced the Red Blend Mountaineer, a blend of over 40% each of Cabernet Sauvignon and Syrah, with small amounts of Petit Verdot and Petite Sirah. Other reds include varietal Syrah, Cabernet Franc, and Grenache. All the reds are Napa Valley AVA. The white is a Chardonnay from Russian River Valley in Sonoma, aged 15% in stainless steel and 85% in barriques. The winery holds back enough wine to offer a rerelease each year of a vintage from ten years or more ago.

Cain Vineyard & Winery

3800 Langtry Road, St. Helena, CA
94574

+1 707 963 1616

Gillian Murphy

winery@cainfive.com

www.cainfive.com

St. Helena AVA

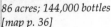

86 acres; 144,000 bottles
[map p. 36]

Cain is located well up Spring Mountain, to the west of St. Helena, with vineyards ranging from 1,400 to 2,100 ft. The Cains bough a 550 acre estate on the mountain in 1980, which had mostly been used as sheep pastures. They planted vineyards and constructed a winery; 1985 was the first vintage for Cain Five (named because it includes the five Bordeaux varieties, Cabernets Sauvignon and Franc, Merlot, Petit Verdot, and Malbec). Cabernet Sauvignon is more than half the plantings. Cain Five remains the flagship wine and is supplemented by Cain Cuvée (a blend of two vintages) and Cain Concept (from purchased grapes). A Sauvignon Blanc was made until 2002 from fruit purchased in Monterey. The winery, including the 2019 and 2020 vintages, burned down in the Glass Fire of 2020.

Carter Cellars

1170 Tubbs Lane, Calistoga, CA
94515

+1 707 445 0311

Mark Carter

info@cartercellars.com

www.cartercellars.com

Calistoga AVA

0 acres; 14,400 bottles
[map p. 36]

Mark Carter founded Carter Cellars when he was running a hotel and restaurant in Eureka, in the far north of California. He commuted to Napa, where Carter Cellars started with the 1998 vintage, made with purchased grapes by winemaker Nils Venge in rented space. In 2006, Mark and Nils started another project, Envy Wines, with a 17 acres vineyard. The wines for Carter Cellars are now made at Envy Wines. Made in small quantities, they come from a roll call of famous vineyards. Almost all the cuvées are single vineyard Cabernet Sauvignons, including six from various Beckstoffer vineyards. The style is full force California.

Charles Krug Winery

2800 Main Street, St. Helena, CA 94574
+1 707 967 2200
info@charleskrug.com
www.charleskrug.com
St. Helena AVA

850 acres; 1,100,000 bottles
[map p. 37]

Charles Krug was one of the first winemakers in Napa Valley, and established a winery in 1861. Cesare and Rosa Mondavi purchased the estate in 1943. They started to produce wines under the Charles Krug label, and in 1946 introduced CK Mondavi as a second, cheaper, line. Other brands are The Divining Rod and Purple Heart Wines . Their sons Peter and Robert took over in 1959 and ran the company until the split in 1966 when Robert left to found his own winery. Peter then ran Charles Krug until his sons, Peter jr. and Marc took over. The wines are reliable, but never achieved the glamour of Robert Mondavi. The large production wines are in general distribution, but in addition, the Limited Release series of eight varietals plus three Cabernet Sauvignon cuvées is available only through the winery. Generations is a Bordeaux blend with 82% Cabernet Sauvignon and 9% each of Merlot and Petit Verdot. A blend from vineyards in Yountville and Howell Mountain, Vintage Selection Cabernet Sauvignon (which includes 1% Petit Verdot) is the top wine. Generations and Vintage Selection both age for 22 months in new barriques. The Redwood Cellar, a six storey building dating from 1872, has been restored to be the tasting room.

Cliff Lede Vineyards

1473 Yountville Cross Road, Yountville, CA 94599
+1 707 944 8642
Karah Gonzalez
info@cliffledevineyards.com
www.cliffledevineyards.com
Stags Leap District AVA

91 acres; 360,000 bottles
[map p. 38]

The winery has had a roll call of famous consultants since it was founded in 2002 when Cliff Lede left his construction business, Ledcor, to go into wine production. David Abreu planted the vineyards, Michel Rolland consulted on winemaking, Philippe Melka was winemaker. Cliff Lede has two major plots in Stags Leap: the 40 acre Twin Peaks Vineyard surrounds the winery on the west side of the Silverado Trail; the 20 acre Poetry Vineyard is higher up on the other side of the Silverado Trail. There's also a 20 acre vineyard at Diamond Mountain in Calistoga. The winery is state of the art, with an optical sorter, gravity feed operations, tronconique tanks for fermentation. Focus is on Cabernet Sauvignon and blends, with several cuvées from different vineyards, the flagship being the Poetry Vineyard cuvée. The Stags Leap Cabernet Sauvignon is the largest production in reds, supplemented by smaller cuvées from Diamond Mountain, Howell Mountain, Songbook (a blend from Thorevilos and Madrona Ranch), Soul Fire (a single-vineyard cuvée from Stags Leap), and Beckstoffer To-Kalon. Claret and High Fidelity are Bordeaux blends. The largest production run is the Sauvignon Blanc, a blend from several vineyards including some Sémillon, aged two thirds in barrique. A separate range, called FEL, comes from Pinot Noir and Chardonnay from a 42 acre vineyard Mendocino County's Anderson Valley to the north. Oenotourism is encouraged by a range of tastings (vineyards are named after rock-and-roll songs, and classic rock plays in the tasting room), and the Poetry Inn is a boutique hotel in the Poetry Vineyard.

Clos Pegase Winery

1060 Dunaweal Lane, Calistoga,
CA 94515
+1 707 942 4981
Leslie Rudd
info@clospegase.com
www.clospegase.com
Calistoga AVA

706 acres; 300,000 bottles
[map p. 36]

This large estate was founded in 1983 when Jan Schrem bought a 50 acre vineyard in Calistoga. It expanded with the purchase of other large vineyards in Napa Valley. The Applebone vineyard surrounds the winery just south of Calistoga, Tenma is north of Calistoga, and Mitsuko's vineyard in Carneros is the largest. A dramatic winery was constructed following an architectural competition, with extensive underground caves excavated from volcanic rock. André Tchelistcheff made the first wines in 1985. The winery and vineyards were purchased in 2013 by Vintage Wine Estates, a holding company owning several other wineries in Napa and Sonoma. The winery was also well known for its art collection, which was not included in the sale. An extensive range of wines includes Napa Cabernet Sauvignon, the single vineyard Hommage Cabernet from Tenma, and Merlot, Pinot Noir, and Malbec varietal wines in reds. Chardonnay and Sauvignon Blanc come from the vineyard in Carneros. Two thirds of production goes into general distribution, and the other third consists of smaller scale projects where the wines can be obtained only at the winery. The winery is into oenotourism with a range of tours and tastings.

Clos du Val Winery

5330 Silverado Trail, Napa, CA
94558
+1 707 259 2200
cmilan@closduval.com
www.closduval.com
Stags Leap District AVA

425 acres; 500,000 bottles
[map p. 39]

Clos du Val classes as an old-line winery in Napa, founded in 1972 by John Goelet and Bernard Portet (son of Château Lafite's technical director), whose aesthetic for winemaking was unsurprisingly French. The style was restrained and the tannins were evident. As Napa turned to riper and riper wines in the late 1990s, the style went out of fashion. This led to a change in approach in the early 2000s, followed more recently by restricting production to estate vineyards, and cutting back the total. From the original 125 acres in Stag's Leap, the flagship Cabernet Sauvignon is smooth and chocolaty. Other wines come from 120 acres in Yountville and 180 acres in Carneros.

Continuum

1677 Sage Canyon Road, St.
Helena, CA 94574
+1 707 944 8100
Tim Mondavi
chelsea@continuumestate.com
www.continuumestate.com
St. Helena AVA

62 acres; 42,000 bottles
[map p. 36]

Michael Mondavi was the winemaker at Robert Mondavi when the winery was sold to Constellation in 2004. He founded Continuum together with other family members shortly after the sale. Unlike Mondavi, which produced wines at all levels, Continuum focuses on the high end. Initially grapes were purchased from the To-Kalon vineyard close to Mondavi, then vineyards were purchased or Pritchard Hill to the east of the valley. By 2012, all grapes came from the estate vineyards. The winery was completed in time for the 2013 harvest. Continuum resembles a left bank Bordeaux blend, with about three quarters Cabernet Sauvignon. The second wine, Novicium, is about half Merlot, with the rest Cabernet Franc and Sauvignon. The style is richer than it was at Mondavi.

Dalla Valle Vineyards

7776 Silverado Trail, Oakville, CA 94562
+1 707 944 2676
Andy Erickson
info@dallavallevineyards.com
www.dallavallevineyards.com
Oakville AVA

22 acres; 36,000 bottles
[map p. 36]

Naoko (originally from a Sake-producing family in Japan) and Gustav Dalla Valle (from a winemaking family in Italy) bought a property on a terrace 400 ft above the Silverado Trail in 1982. It came with a 3 acre vineyard, they purchased more land from neighboring properties, built a winery, and hired Heidi Barret as winemaker for the first vintage in 1986. Gustav died in 1995 and Naoko continued. The specialty is Cabernet Franc—"all our wines are blended with Cabernet Franc," says Naoko. The flagship wine, Maya (only 500 cases) is a roughly equal blend of Cabernet Franc and Cabernet Sauvignon. The varietal Cabernet Sauvignon has a small proportion of Cabernet Franc; MDV is a cuvée from the best block of Cabernet Sauvignon. The latest cuvée is a second wine, Collina, coming from younger vines and intended to be more approachable.

Dana Estates

1500 Whitehall Ln, St Helena, CA 94574
+1 707 963 4365
Brigid Babb
inquiries@danaestates.com
danaestates.com
Rutherford AVA

59 acres; 26,000 bottles [map p. 37]

The property has made wine under various names, starting before Prohibition. The modern era started with Livingston Vineyards in 1984. Later the name changed to Livingston-Moffet. Grapes for the brand came from the property, but the wine was actually made elsewhere. South Korean businessman Hi Sang Lee (one of South Korea's largest importers of fine wine) bought the property in 2005. Philippe Melka is the consulting winemaker. The 8 acre Helms Vineyard is part of the 30 acre estate on the Rutherford Bench. There are also vineyards across the valley. The 35 acre Hershey Vineyard is at 1,800 foot elevation on Howell Mountain. The Lotus Vineyard is at 1,200 foot just below the Howell Mountain AVA, and Crystal Vineyard is just below it at 800 foot altitude. A 100% Cabernet Sauvignon is produced from each vineyard, aged for 21 months entirely in new oak. A Sauvignon Blanc, aged entirely in new oak, comes from Hershey Vineyard. The largest release, about half of production, is Onda, a blend with 95% Cabernet Sauvignon, 4% Merlot, and 1% Petit Verdot, sourced two-thirds from Crystal Springs Vineyard with the rest from the other vineyards. There is also a second label, VASO Cellars, sold only in South Korea until 2013, which produces wines at a lower price point, principally from Hershey Vineyard.

Darioush Winery

4240 Silverado Trail, Napa, CA 94558
+1 707 257 2345
Darioush Khaledi
info@darioush.com
www.darioush.com
Oak Knoll AVA

121 acres; 120,000 bottles [map p. 39]

Darioush Khaledi came from Iran in 1976 and built a major grocery chain before he purchased the Altamura winery in 1997. Five years later, a new winery opened, with a striking expression of the Persian aesthetic modeled on Persepolis, with an entrance through reflecting pools and columns. A visit here is as much about the experience as about the wines, which are usually described as Bordeaux-style. The Signature Cabernet Sauvignon comes from (relatively) cooler hillside sites around Napa Valley. It's usually around 83% Cabernet Sauvignon, 10% Merlot, and small amounts of Cabernet Franc, Malbec, and Petit Verdot, aged in mostly new barriques. The Merlot is 90-100% varietal. Other varietals in the Signature range include Syrah (labeled Shiraz here), Cabernet Franc, and Malbec, as well as Chardonnay and Pinot Noir from Russian River. The top cuvée is the Darius II Cabernet Sauvignon (80% Cabernet Sauvignon with Merlot and Cabernet Franc). The Caravan cuvée is what passes for entry-level here, with 60% Cabernet Sauvignon and 20% each of Cabernet Franc and Merlot, aged in 70% new barriques.

Del Dotto Vineyards

1445 St Helena Hwy, St Helena,
CA 94574
+1 707 963 2134
mail@deldottovineyards.com
www.deldottovineyards.com

St. Helena AVA

74 acres; 30,000 bottles
[map p. 37]

Dave Del Dotto 's experience in real estate and TV is reflected in the three Del Dotto wineries. The historical winery and caves is on Atlas Peak Road in Napa, and has aging cellars constructed in 1885. The current winery is a fake Italian palace south of St. Helena, built in 2007, where the caves are lined with Italian marble and ancient tiles depicting the history of wine. Piazza del Dotto just north of Yountville is another building in Italian style Tastings and tours and available at all three locations, with the emphasis as much on the experience as the wine. Del Dotto's focus is on Cabernet Sauvignon, with a large number of different cuvées from eight vineyards all around the valley, some produced in very small amounts. There are also cuvées from the Villa del Lago winery on Pritchard Hill. All wines age 100% new oak, but there's experimentation with different types of oak, often shown off by examples in the tastings. In addition, Pinot Noir, Chardonnay, and other varieties come from 40 acres of vineyards at the Cinghiale Ranch on Sonoma Coast.

Duckhorn Vineyards

1000 Lodi Lane, St. Helena, CA
94574
+1 707 963 7108
reservations@duckhorn.com
www.duckhorn.com

St. Helena AVA

551 acres; 1,000,000 bottles
[map p. 37]

Founded by Dan and Margaret Duckhorn in 1976, the estate was one of the first in the establishment of modern Napa Valley, starting with a 10 acre property in St. Helena. The distinctive feature was a focus on Merlot rather than the Cabernet Sauvignon emphasized by virtually all other producers. The range of Merlot extends from the Napa Valley cuvée to five single-vineyard cuvées, ranging from Atlas Peak to Carneros. The flagship is the Three Palms Merlot, from a vineyard at the east side of the valley just south of Calistoga. After Merlot, Bordeaux blends, Sauvignon Blanc, and Chardonnay followed. Duckhorn was sold in 2007 to a venture capital firm, GI partners, which expanded the business before selling in 2016 to another venture capital firm, TSG Consumer Partners. By then, Duckhorn had a portfolio including several other wineries—Paraduxx in Napa, Goldeneye in Mendocino, and Canvasback in Washington being the most distinguished. Since the latest takeover, the portfolio has expanded further by purchasing Calera in Mount Harlan, and Kosta Browne in Sonoma. Duckhorn itself remains under the same winemaking team.

Ehlers Estate

3222 Ehlers Lane, St. Helena, CA
94574
+1 707 963 5972
Kevin Morrisey
info@ehlersestate.com
www.ehlersestate.com

St. Helena AVA

40 acres; 96,000 bottles
[map p. 37]

Just north of St. Helena, Ehlers Estate takes it name from Bernard Ehlers, who founded a winery there in 1856. Wineries of several different names occupied the space, until in 2001 the property was sold to Jean and Sylvaine Leducq. Since their deaths it has been owned by the Leducq Foundation, with profits going to cardiovascular research. The tasting room is in an old stone building from the nineteenth century—a 'ghost winery' in the local vernacular. Wines include Sauvignon Blanc in Fumé Blanc style (aged for 6 months in barrique), a varietal Cabernet Franc (aged for 22 months in 50% new French barriques), Portrait Red Blend (38% Cabernet Sauvignon, 34% Cabernet Franc, and 28% Merlot aged in barriques with 40% new oak), and a range of Cabernet Sauvignons. There's a Napa Valley cuvée, the J. Leducq cuvée from a single parcel, and the top of the line 1886 Cabernet Sauvignon, 100% varietal, selected from several blocks and distinguished by pewter packaging and platinum etching.

Favia Erickson

PO Box 6978, Napa, CA 94558
+1 707 256 0875
Annie Favia & Andy Erickson
info@faviawines.com
www.faviawine.com
Napa Valley AVA

0 acres; 24,000 bottles [map p. 39]

Favia Erickson is the winery of Andy Erickson and his wife Annie Favia. Andy made wine with several well-known winemakers, including John Kongsgaard, before becoming the winemaker at Staglin, and now consults for many producers in the valley. Annie worked as a viticulturalist with David Abreu before turning to work full time at Favia Erickson. They founded Favia in 2003, and in 2018 they moved to Coombsville, where they live in a renovated old building dating from 1886, with a stone cellar on the ground floor for winemaking. They describe Favia as the only boutique wine and tea producer in Napa, referring to a second project in which they produce herbal teas. There have been many different cuvées over the years, with different varieties from different sources, but the two most conventional varietals are the Coombsville and Oakville Cabernet Sauvignon and Cabernet Franc. The flagship wine is the Cerro Sur, a blend of about 85% Cabernet Franc with Cabernet Sauvignon, sourced from old vines at a high elevation vineyard in Wooden Valley to the east of the valley. A Chardonnay comes from the vineyard around the house; malolactic fermentation is blocked, and it ages in used barriques. Rhone-style wines come from grapes sourced from the Shake Ridge Vineyard an Amador County. The entry-level wines are called Room (with releases in both red and white that change each year) and Carbone (a blend of 61% Cabernet Franc, 27% Cabernet Sauvignon, and 11% Petit Verdot from the estate vineyards, named for the original owners of the property). If there's a favorite grape variety at Favia Erickson, it's Cabernet Franc. Production is usually less than 300 cases of each wine.

Flora Springs Winery

1978 W. Zinfandel Lane, St. Helena, CA 94574
+1 707 963 5711
info@florasprings.com
www.florasprings.com
St. Helena AVA

499 acres; 240,000 bottles [map p. 37]

It is hard to miss the Flora Springs tasting room as you drive up route 29 into St. Helena and see a striking building with an undulating roof. (They call it The Room.) The winery is up the hill at the end of Zinfandel Lane, and was where the venture started when Jerry and Flora Komes bought an old winery property in 1978 as a place to retire. Now in the third generation, Flora Springs has become one of the largest properties in Napa still in family hands. The wide range of wines extends from the standard Napa Valley varietals, to the flagship Trilogy, a blend of Cabernet Sauvignon with about 10% each of Malbec and Petit Verdot. There are also wines produced in smaller quantities and available only from the wine club or at the tasting room.

Forman Vineyards

1501 Big Rock Rd., St. Helena, CA 94574
+1 707 963 3900
Ric Forman
info@formanvineyard.com
www.formanvineyard.com
St. Helena AVA

25 acres; 30,000 bottles [map p. 36]

Ric Forman has been involved in making wine in Napa Valley since the start of the modern era, beginning at Stony Hill, Sterling (where he established its reputation when he was its winemaker), and Newton (which he was involved in founding), before founding his own estate in St. Helena at the base of Howell Mountain in 1978, where the land had to be dynamited to plant the vines. His winemaking was influenced by time spent in Bordeaux; the Cabernet Sauvignon is a blend, usually with just over 75% Cabernet Sauvignon, and Merlot, Cabernet Franc, and Petit Verdot, aged in 75% new oak. The wines were known for their more European style until a transition to later picking after 2003, partly due to Ric's son Toby joining the winery. His objective with Chardonnay, which comes from Rutherford, is to achieve a leaner, Chablis-like style, and it is produced with no malolactic fermentation.

Freemark Abbey

3022 St. Helena Highway North,
St. Helena, CA 94574
+1 800 963 9698
Ted Edwards
info@freemarkabbey.com
www.freemarkabbey.com
St. Helena AVA

🚶 $35 🏭 🚜 🛢 🚜

0 acres; 720,000 bottles
[map p. 37]

This venerable property dates from 1881. It took its present name in 1939 after a change of ownership. The modern era started when a group bought it in 1967 and focused on Cabernet Sauvignon. It was sold to an investor group in 2001, and then became part of Jackson Family Estates in 2006. The historic stone building was handsomely restored in 2016, and is open for a range of tours and tastings. Ted Edwards has been the winemaker since 1986. Freemark Abbey does not own vineyards, but sources fruit from growers, often on long term contracts. It is best known for its flagship Cabernet from the 22 acre Bosché vineyard on the Rutherford Bench (made since 1970). It usually has up to 18% Merlot and production is less than 4,000 cases. I find this to offer one of the more European styles in Napa. The Chardonnay is known for its restrained style, emphasizing freshness by no malolactic fermentation, and limiting oak. Unusually for Napa, the winery also has a restaurant, open for lunch.

Frog's Leap Winery

8815 Conn Creek Rd, Rutherford,
CA 94573
+1 707 963 4704
John Williams
ribbit@frogsleap.com
www.frogsleap.com
Rutherford AVA

❗ $35 🏭 🚜 🛢 🚜

580 acres; 60,000 bottles
[map p. 38]

John Williams founded Frog's Leap together with Larry Turley in 1981 after making wine at Stag's Leap. The first releases were made from purchased grapes. Larry left to form Turley Wine Cellars, and John acquired the winery site in 1994: it was originally the site of the Adamson Winery in 1884, and the large red barn was refurbished to become Frog's Leap Winery. The home vineyard of 40 acres surrounds the winery, which also owns 88 acres in Rutherford as well as farming another 100 acres. The vineyards are dry farmed. The name is followed by a slightly zany approach, so tours can be slightly different here. Unusually for Napa, the focus was originally on Sauvignon Blanc and Zinfandel: Cabernet Sauvignon and other varieties followed as the estate vineyards came on line, but Sauvignon Blanc is still the flagship wine.

Futo Wines

1575 Oakville Grade, Oakville, CA
94558
+1 707 944 9333
Tom & Kyle Futo
info@futowines.com
www.futowines.com
Oakville AVA

❗ @ 🚜 🚜

27 acres; 20,000 bottles
[map p. 38]

Brothers Tom and Kyle Futo bought the 40 acre property of Oakford Vineyards with 7 acres of vineyards in 2002, in the hills of Mount Veeder overlooking Oakville. In 2004 they added an adjacent lot, and in 2008 they built the winery. In 2011 they purchased a property in Stags Leap with a 5 acre vineyard of Cabernet Sauvignon. There are three cuvées. Futo Oakville is a Bordeaux blend with about 70% Cabernet Sauvignon from the estate in Oakville. Futo 5500 is a Cabernet Sauvignon (97% varietal with the rest being Merlot) from the Stags Leap property. The wines age in 70% new oak. OV was started as a second label from the Oakville Estate, but then in 2012 fruit was added from the Stags Leap vineyard, and it was renamed OV|SL. It remains a Bordeaux blend, with just under 70% Cabernet Sauvignon. The wines acquired cult status so rapidly that there was a waiting list for the first release.

Gallica

3125 N St. Helena Highway, St. Helena, CA 94574

+1 707 963 1096

Rosemary Cakebread

info@gallicawine.com

www.gallicawine.com

St. Helena AVA

2 acres; 12,000 bottles

[map p. 37]

Rosemary Cakebread started making wine at Inglenook, after graduating from UC Davis in oenology. She was the winemaker for Spottswoode from 1997 to 2005. (She worked briefly at Cakebread Cellars and is married to Bruce Cakebread.) She started Gallica Cellars in 2007, and makes wine from a mix of estate and purchased grapes from various sources. The flagship wine is Cabernet Sauvignon from Oakville, but she also produces wines from Rhône varieties, including Grenache from Sonoma and from Amador, Syrah from Santa Lucia Highlands, as well as Albariño from the Sierra Foothills.

Gemstone Vineyard

PO Box 3477, Yountville, CA 94599

+1 707 944 0944

Amy Marks Dornbusch

info@gemstonewine.com

www.gemstonevineyard.com

Yountville AVA

17 acres; 20,000 bottles

[map p. 38]

The name reflects Suzie and Paul Frank's former business in Los Angeles, in diamonds, before they purchased the vineyard in Yountville in 1997. The vineyard was entirely planted to Chardonnay, but over time the Franks replanted almost completely with Cabernet Sauvignon and small amounts of the other Bordeaux varieties. The Franks sold the estate in 2008 to Carole and Michael Marks from Silicon Valley. Philippe Melka was winemaker from 2005, until Thomas Rivers Brown, known for making many cult wines, took over. The vineyard is divided into 20 small blocks, each of which is vinified separately. The Estate Red is a blend with about 70% Cabernet Sauvignon and 20% Merlot. Three Cabernet Sauvignon cuvées are 100% varietal: Heritage includes all of the 16 clones planted in the vineyard, Alluvial Selection comes from upper blocks on the alluvial fan, and Ruby is a selection of four top barrels.

Hyde de Villaine Wines

588 Trancas Street, Napa, CA 94558

+1 707 251 9121

Nate Oliver

nate@hdvwines.com

www.hdvwines.com

Napa Valley AVA

27 acres; 54,000 bottles

[map p. 39]

The name HdV (more fully Hyde de Villaine Wines) reflects the partnership between Larry Hyde (of the Hyde Ranch in Carneros) and Aubert de Villaine (of Domaine de la Romanée Conti). There is a family relationship, as Aubert's wife, Pamela, is Larry's cousin. Larry started Hyde Vineyard in 1979, and now with 200 acres of vineyards it is one of the top sources for grapes from Carneros. The grapes for HdV originally came only from Hyde Vineyard. "This is a very small family venture, based on the idea of making the best possible wines from the Hyde Vineyard," Aubert said. The project started in 2000, and the winery was built in 2003, a practical building with the appearance of warehouse. The focus is on Pinot Noir and Chardonnay, but in 2016 HdV purchased the parcel on which the winery stands, which has a 24 acre vineyard of Syrah, which has been replanted with other varieties in order to expand the range. Winemaker Stephane Vivier calls the stylistic objective 'restrained opulence.' Fruit is pressed very slowly, there is full malolactic fermentation, and the wine ages in barriques with no battonage, and no fining or filtration before bottling.

The Hess Collection

4411 Redwood Road, Napa, CA 94558
+1 707 255 1144
Timothy & Sabrina Persson
info@hesscollection.com
hesscollection.com
Mount Veeder AVA

687 acres; 7,200,000 bottles
[map p. 39]

The Hess Collection refers both to wine production and to the contemporary art collection at the museum next to the winery. Donald Hess, who comes from a family of beer brewers in Switzerland, created his vineyard about 2000 feet up Mount Veeder in 1978. The winery used to be one of the facilities used by the Christian Brothers. Hess is a very large producer, with several other wineries, and The Hess Collection represents about 10% of all production, concentrating on estate wines from Mount Veeder. The wines are well made, in a soft, crowd-pleasing style. Hess Select wines are made at a winery in American Canyon in southern Napa County.

Hourglass Wine Company

701 Lommel Road, Calistoga, CA 94515
+1 707 968 9332
Jeff Smith
marybeth@hourglasswine.com
www.hourglasswine.com
Calistoga AVA

25 acres; 54,000 bottles
[map p. 37]

Ned Smith bought a 6 acre parcel on Lodi Lane in 1976. It's called the Hourglass Vineyard because it's at the most constricted point of Napa Valley. Originally Ned and his son Jeff planted Zinfandel, but when it became necessary to replant in the 1990s, it was replaced by Cabernet Sauvignon. The Smiths bought the Blueline Vineyard, south of Calistoga, in 2006, and replanted it with Cabernet Sauvignon, Cabernet Franc, and Merlot. Bob Foley was the winemaker. The Hourglass Estate Cabernet Sauvignon is 100% varietal, from the Hourglass vineyard. From the Blueline Estate there are varietal Cabernet Sauvignon, Cabernet Franc, Merlot, and Malbec cuvées. There's also a Cabernet and Petit Verdot blend, the HGIII blend that includes some Italian varieties, and a Sauvignon Blanc (the only white wine). The Hourglass winery and guest house were destroyed in the Glass Fire of 2020.

Hundred Acre Vineyard

1345 Railroad Avenue, St. Helena, CA 94574
+1 707 967 9398
Jeanine Aitken
info@hundredacre.com
www.hundredacre.com
St. Helena AVA

30 acres; 12,000 bottles
[map p. 37]

Investment banker Jayson Woodbridge founded Hundred Acre in 2000 with the purchase of the 10 acre Kayli Morgan vineyard on the Silverado Trail between St. Helena and Calistoga. He subsequently purchased the 15 acre Ark vineyard on Howell Mountain, followed by the Few and Far Between parcel just above the Eisele vineyard. Each produces a 100% Cabernet Sauvignon in full-force style—needless to say, in 100% new oak—often with alcohol above 15%. The winery was constructed under the Ark vineyard in 2005. Philippe Melka made the initial vintages in 2000 and 2001, after which Jayson took over. Under the general rubric of One True Vine, Jayson also owns several other producers, making wines in more popular styles in California and Italy.

The Kapcsándy Family Winery

1001 State Lane, Yountville, CA 94599
+1 707 948 3100
Brittany McKahn
info@kapcsandywines.com
www.kapcsandywines.com
Yountville AVA

15 acres; 24,000 bottles
[map p. 39]

Lou Kapcsándy and his family purchased the State Lane Vineyard in Yountville, which had previously been the source for Beringer's Private Reserve Cabernet Sauvignon, in 2000, and replanted the vineyard in 2002. The winery was built in 2005. A self-confessed Francophile, his wines are intended to follow Bordeaux. "We dislike high-alcohol wines," he says, "Most of the wines we make have less than 14% alcohol." Nonetheless, the style tends to be powerful. Denis Malbec from Château Latour was the winemaker until he died in an accident in 2016. The flagship wine is the so-called Grand Vin, the State Lane Cabernet Sauvignon (90-99% Cabernet). The Estate Cuvée is a more typical Bordeaux blend, with about two thirds Cabernet Sauvignon. Roberta's Reserve is a 100% Merlot. Rhapsodia is a right-bank blend, two thirds Cabernet Franc to one third Merlot.

Kenzo Estate

3200 Monticello Road, Napa, CA 94558
+1 707 254 7572
Tamamo Dughman
info@kenzoestate.com
www.kenzoestate.com
Napa Valley AVA

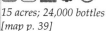

151 acres; 200,000 bottles
[map p. 39]

Kenzo Tsujimoto is Chairman of Japan's Capcom Group, a gaming company that produces the Street Fighter and Resident Evil video games. In 1990, he purchased 4,000 acres of an old equestrian ranch on Mount George. He had not originally intended to make wine, but in 2002 he brought in an all-star team and planted a vineyard, with David Abreu as the vineyard manager and Heidi Barrett as the consulting winemaker. The tasting room offers pairings of the wines with food created by Thomas Keller of the French Laundry. There are four wines: Rindo (the nearest thing to an entry-level wine) and Murasaki are Cabernet-based blends, Ai is a varietal Cabernet Sauvignon, and Asatsuyu is a Sauvignon Blanc. The winery was followed by a Japanese restaurant in downtown Napa, also called Kenzo.

La Jota Vineyard

1102 Las Posadas Road, Angwin, CA 94508
3299 Bennett Lane, Calistoga CA 94515 (tasting room)
+1 877 222 0292
Chris Carpenter
info@lajotavineyardco.com
www.lajotavineyardco.com
Howell Mountain AVA

27 acres; 42,000 bottles
[map p. 36]

La Jota is a boutique winery producing wines from two vineyards: the La Jota vineyard that surrounds the winery, which was built in 1898; and the W. S. Keyes vineyard a mile away, both on Howell Mountain between 1,700 and 1,900 ft elevation. The modern incarnation of La Jota dates from 1982; the Smiths who founded it sold to Markham Vineyards in 2001, who in turn sold it to Jackson Family Estates in 2003. La Jota produces varietal Cabernet Sauvignon and Cabernet Franc; the varietal Merlot comes from the W. S. Keyes vineyard. The wines are rich but not overpowering: Cabernet Sauvignon is the most forceful, Cabernet Franc is smoother with a touch of tobacco, Merlot has the most aromatic lift and ends in bitter chocolate. They can be tasted at another Jackson property, Spire Collection near Calistoga.

112

Lagier Meredith Vineyard

4967 Dry Creek Road, Napa, CA 94558
+1 707 253 0653
Carole Meredith
mail@lagiermeredith.com
www.lagiermeredith.com
Yountville AVA

🚫 🏭 🍇 🌿

5 acres; 8,000 bottles
[map p. 38]

Carole Meredith and Steve Lagier bought the property, located at 1300 foot elevation on Mount Veeder on one of the routes across the mountain between Napa and Sonoma, to be their home in 1986. Steve worked at Robert Mondavi until 1999, and Carol was a Professor at UC Davis, working on the genetics of grapevines until 2003. The property came with a small area that had been cleared, which they eventually turned into a vineyard, starting with Syrah in 1994, later adding Zinfandel (for which Carole had identified the origins by DNA fingerprinting) and the less common varieties of Malbec and Mondeuse. All the wines are aged in old barriques. This is one of the smallest (and most artisanal) wineries in Napa, and the wines are mostly sold directly to consumers.

Lail Vineyards

320 Stone Ridge Road, Angwin, CA 94508
+1 707 968 9900
Chantal Leruitte
info@lailvineyards.com
www.lailvineyards.com
Howell Mountain AVA

📦 🏭 🍇 🛢 🚜

7 acres; 48,000 bottles [map p. 36]

Robin Lail has a long history in Napa Valley. The daughter of John Daniels, who inherited Inglenook, she was a partner in the creation of Dominus. She founded her own estate in 19977, when she purchased a 20 acre property on Howell Mountain. Grapes come from two vineyards: the 2.6 acres Totem Vineyard in Yountville was part of the original Inglenook estate; and the 3 acre Mole Hill vineyard, where the winery is located, is about 1,700 ft up Howell Mountain. Fruit is also purchased from the Heimark Vineyard (between Angwin and Calistoga). The flagship wine is the J. Daniel Cuvée, which is a Cabernet Sauvignon from various sources, as also is the Blueprint Cabernet (produced in larger amounts). J. Daniel started with fruit from Yountville and Oakville, before switching to mountain sources. It's a powerful wine, and since the Heimark fruit was added in 2008, its alcohol level has increased to over 15%. New oak is 75-80%. Mole Hill Cabernet Sauvignon is a single vineyard release. There are two Sauvignon Blancs: Blueprint is aged in stainless steel and aims for crispness, whereas Georgia is aged entirely in new oak. The grapes for Georgia come from the Totem vineyard. Philippe Melka is the winemaker. As an alternative to going up the mountain to the winery, the wines can be tasted at Maisonry in Yountville.

Laird Family Estate

5055 Solano Ave, Napa, CA 94558
+1 707 257 0360
Clarke Knippen
info@lairdfamilyestate.com
www.lairdfamilyestate.com
Napa Valley AVA

🚶 🏭 🍇 🚜

2401 acres; 120,000 bottles
[map p. 39]

One of the largest grape growers in Napa Valley, Laird sells grapes to more than 60 wineries. The company has been selling grapes since 1970, but made its first wine only in 1999, with Paul Hobbs as winemaker. Brian Mox came as winemaker in 2015. Laird also has a custom crush facility, with a capacity for handling more than 400,000 cases, which is used by more than 60 wineries. This is a far cry from the start, when Ken Laird (originally a mechanical engineer) bought an abandoned fruit orchard in Calistoga and planted vines. He sold the grapes to Robert Mondavi. Today has daughter Rebecca manages the winery and her brother Justin manages the vineyards. The winery is known for its pyramidal shape, and it has one of the most popular tasting rooms in Napa. Laird's wines are made from only about 3% of their vineyards, all in an immediately approachable style. The wines are almost all single varietals, including Cabernet Sauvignon, Pinot Noir, Malbec, Syrah, Red Chardonnay, Pinot Grigio, and Sauvignon Blanc .

Lokoya

3787 Spring Mountain Road, St.
Helena CA 94574
+1 707 948 1968
Bradley Wasserman
info@lokoya.com
www.lokoya.com
St. Helena AVA

25 acres; 24,000 bottles
[map p. 36]

Lokoya is not so much a winery as a boutique brand name created in 1995 within Jackson Family Estates for a collection of varietal Cabernet Sauvignons from different mountain appellations: Mount Veeder, Howell Mountain, Diamond Mountain, and Spring Mountain. Chris Carpenter, who also makes the wines for another boutique operation within Jackson, La Jota Vineyard, is the winemaker. The style is similar: dense and rich, full of flavor but not overpowering, although with a marked tannic presence. The winery on Spring Mountain Road is a historic building, purchased by Jackson in 2013 and renovated in 2017, and the wines can be tasted there.

Long Meadow Ranch

738 Main St, St Helena, CA 94574
+1 707 963 4555
Chris Hall
info@longmeadowranch.com
www.longmeadowranch.com
St. Helena AVA

89 acres; 900,000 bottles
[map p. 37]

Ted Hall worked at McKinsey, but had a history in wine management—he was Chairman of Robert Mondavi when it was sold to Constellation—when he bought Long Meadow Ranch in 1989. Following the model of polyculture, with livestock and other crops as well as viticulture, this is a family-run operation, now run by Ted's son Christopher. Vineyards are in three properties, the farmstead in St. Helena (on route 29 just south of the town, where there is a tasting room and restaurant)), an estate in Rutherford about four miles to the south, which has 74 acres of vines, and a property in the Mayacamas mountains, where the winery is located, surrounded by 16 acres of vines. There's also a 69 acre estate and tasting room in Mendocino's Anderson Valley to the north, planted with Pinot Noir, Pinot Gris, and Chardonnay. The Rutherford estate produces Cabernet Sauvignon, Merlot, and Sauvignon Blanc; at Mayacamas there are also the less common varieties of Cabernet Franc and Sangiovese. Long Meadow is known for a relatively restrained style of Cabernet Sauvignon, which makes it fitting that in 2018 they purchased Stony Hill Vineyard (see mini-profile), known for an elegant approach to Chardonnay. The two producers continue to function separately.

Madrigal Vineyards

3718 N. St. Helena Hwy, P.O. Box 937,
Calistoga, CA 94515
+1 707 942 8619
Chris Madrigal
tastingroom@madrigalfamilywinery.com
www.madrigalfamilywinery.com
St. Helena AVA

40 acres; 72,000 bottles
[map p. 36]

The Madrigal family came from Mexico and started farming in Napa Valley in the 1940s. Jess Madrigal started a vineyard management company in 1984, and his son Chris founded the winery in 1995. Wines were made at a custom crush facility until the winery was built in 2007. There's something of a focus here on unusual varieties, with cuvées of Grenache, Tempranillo, Petite Syrah, and Petit Verdot, as well as Zinfandel, Cabernet Franc, and Cabernet Sauvignon. There is a tasting room in Sausalito, as well as at the winery in Napa. Venture Capital firm Bacchus Capital Management has a part share in the winery.

Marciano Estate

2401 Sulphur Springs Ave, St Helena, CA 94574
+1 707 967 0983
Adrien Signorello
info@marcianoestate.com
www.marcianoestate.com
St. Helena AVA

10 acres; 14,000 bottles [map p. 37]

This property originated as the Madroño Estate, engaged in polyculture and owned by the Bourne family until the 1950s when it was sold to Christian Brothers to be used as retreat. The Bradley family bought the property in 1994 and planted 20 acres of grapevines grapes, and the grapes were sold. Maurice Marciano, a cofounder of the Guess Inc. clothing brand, bought the property in 2006. He halved the vineyard area (planting olive trees in place of some of the plots), hired David Abreu to manage the vineyards, and built a winery including a striking circular barrel room. Winemaker Morgan Maureze came at the start of the project. The Cabernet Sauvignon is 85% Cabernet Sauvignon. 10% Cabernet Franc, and 5% Petit Verdot. There is also a Kosher wine that is 100% Cabernet Sauvignon, and a non-mevushal wine for Passover. The M Proprietary Red is a blend of Cabernet Sauvignon and Cabernet Franc. Coming from a single acre of Sauvignon Blanc and Sauvignon Musqé, the Sauvignon Blanc is a halfway house in style, aged in a mix of new barriques, old barriques, stainless steel, and concrete. Maurice Marciano owns Wally's wine store in Los Angeles (together with his brothers), and the wines can be purchased there, as well as from the estate.

Markham Vineyards

2812 St. Helena Hwy. North, PO 636, St. Helena, CA 94574
+1 707 963 5292
Jake Hajer
admin@markhamvineyards.com
www.markhamvineyards.com
St. Helena AVA

351 acres; 1,300,000 bottles [map p. 37]

This was originally the Laurent Winery, founded in 1874; after a series of changes in ownership, it became a cooperative, and ended up with Heublein, who sold it to Bruce Markham in 1977. Bruce produced wine for a decade and then sold the winery to the Mercian Corporation, a Japanese wine producer that is now part of the Kirin beer company. Markham was transferred to another part of Kirin, Distinguished Vineyards, which also owns Textbook in Napa. Expanded after Mercian's purchase, this is now a very large operation. There's a wide range of wines at entry-level for Napa, with Merlot a prominent part; the mid-level range, called Heritage Selection, consisting of several monovarietals, and the releases of single-vineyard Cabernet Sauvignon or Merlot, are available only at the winery.

Materra Cunat Family Vineyards

4326 Big Ranch Road, Napa, California
+1 707 224 4900
Harry Heitz
info@materrawines.com
www.materrawines.com
Oak Knoll AVA

40 acres; 42,000 bottles [map p. 39]

When Brian and Miki Cunat bought this 50 acre property in the Oak Knoll District in 2007, it was planted entirely with 40 acres of Merlot. They diversified the varieties by planting Chardonnay, Sauvignon Blanc, and Viognier. The winery was completed in 2015, and offers a custom crush facility as well as making the estate wines. Merlot is 99% of the Oak Knoll Right Bank cuvée. Cunat Reserve is a selection of the best Merlot, blended with 10% Cabernet Sauvignon. Midnight is an unusual blend of 65% Petit Verdot, 32% Malbec, and 3% Merlot. The four Cabernet Sauvignon releases (varying from 92-99% Cabernet Sauvignon) draw on purchased fruit: Hidden Block (Napa Valley AVA), Diamond Mountain, Howell Mountain, and 1856 (from Oak Knoll). All the red wines age for 22 months in barriques, usually with about 85% new oak. Reds represent about 40% of production. The 60% of whites are divided into three varietal wines, Chardonnay, Sauvignon Blanc, and Viognier, at a much lower price point than the reds.

Maybach Family Vineyards

3730 Silverado Trail, St. Helena, CA 94562
+1 415 668 8685
Thomas Brown
info@maybachwine.com
www.maybachwine.com
Oakville AVA

12,000 bottles

Maybach is a famous name in engineering, and the Maybach family in Napa are the great grandchildren of Wilhelm Maybach, an inventor of the internal combustion engine. The winery was founded in 2004. Although the address is in Oakville, production is actually split between Napa and Sonoma, with the Cabernet Sauvignons coming from Napa (Materium from a single vineyard at 1000 foot elevation above Oakville, and Amoenus from the western side of Calistoga), while the Imgard Pinot Noir and Eterium Chardonnay come from Sonoma Coast. Materium is the flagship, and ages in 100% new French oak. The winemaker is famed Thomas Rivers Brown, and the style is powerful.

Melka Estates

2900 Silverado Trail N, St. Helena, CA 94574
+1 707 963 6008
Cherie & Phllipe Melka
info@melkaestates.com
www.melkaestates.com
St. Helena AVA

25 acres; 36,000 bottles
[map p. 37]

Philippe Melka is a famous winemaker in Napa Valley, where he has been involved in making cult wines for many producers. He started when he came from Bordeaux to study the soils at Dominus, when he met his wife, Cherie. They founded Melka Estates in 1996, making the CJ and Métisse blends from grapes sourced in the valley. In 2003, they stopped making the Métisse Proprietary Red, and switched to several single-vineyard wines: Jumping Goat and Martinez are Bordeaux blends. In 2001, they purchased a vineyard in Knights Valley, just north of Napa Valley in Sonoma. Above the fog line, the vineyard makes four Mekerra cuvées. The Proprietary Red is a more or less equal blend of Cabernet Franc and Merlot, and there are Merlot, Chardonnay, and a Sauvignon Blanc from a 2300 foot high plot In 2011, they purchased a vineyard just outside St. Helena, and in 2016 they converted a barn on the property into a winery. This is the source for the Métisse Montbleau Vineyard Cabernet Sauvignon. Majestique is used for a small range of single vineyard wines from sources outside Napa Valley.

Mending Wall Winery

3730 Silverado Trail N, St Helena, CA 94574
+1 707 709 4200
Thomas Rivers Brown
info@mendingwall.com
www.mendingwall.com
St. Helena AVA

5 acres; 30,000 bottles
[map p. 37]

Established in 2014, this venture is a partnership between Frank Dotzler (of Outpost Winery), Mark Pulido and Donna Walker (of Pulido-Walker Wine) and flying winemaker Thomas Brown. The focus is on Cabernet Sauvignon, sourced from top sites in Napa Valley: there's a Napa Valley release, and two wines from single vineyards, Oakville Ranch and Tournahu (a 7 acre plot in Saint Helena). The Petite Sirah comes from the Carver Sutro vineyard in the Palisades. Mortar & Stone is a blend of Petite Sirah and Zinfandel introduced in 2017; and the white Stone & Stone, a blend of Sauvignon Blanc and Sémillon where malolactic fermentation is blocked, was added the same year. Brown Ranch Chardonnay comes from a single site in Carneros. Production levels are low, even the Napa Valley Cabernet Sauvignon is rarely more than 500 cases, and most of the others are around 100 cases, and wines are sold only directly through the winery, mostly by mailing list.

Merryvale Wines

1000 Main Street, St. Helena, CA 94574
+1 707 963 7777
René Schlatter
tastingroom@merryvale.com
www.merryvale.com
St. Helena AVA

74 acres; 180,000 bottles
[map p. 37]

On route 29 through St. Helena, Merryvale was one of the first wineries built after Prohibition, in 1933. It passed through various hands until Jack Schlatter became a partner and the name changed to Merryvale in 1991. The Schlatter family became sole owners in 1996; Jack continues to spend time in Switzerland, where the family comes from, and his son René took over the winery in 2008. The 25 acre Profile Estate Vineyard east of St. Helena, which is the source for the flagship Profile red Bordeaux blend, the F1 block Cabernet Sauvignon, and the Silhouette Chardonnay, was purchased in 1997. Under the Merryvale label there's a wide range of wines, including the Napa Valley Cabernet Sauvignon (sourced from three separate vineyards), varietal Merlot and Malbec. Pinot Noir and Chardonnay come from Carneros, including a Chardonnay from the Hyde Vineyard. A lower-level range of wines uses the Starmont label.

Mount Veeder Winery

1999 Mount Veeder Road, Napa, CA 94558
+1 707 967 3830
Janet Myers
customerservice@mtveeder.com
www.mtveeder.com
Mount Veeder AVA

47 acres; 240,000 bottles
[map p. 39]

Mount Veeder was one of the first mountain wineries in Napa Valley, with its inaugural Cabernet Sauvignon released in 1973. The story goes that it started by accident, when a neighbor gave Michael Bernstein some grapevine cuttings, and after he stuck them in the ground, they grew. Plantings later expanded into three vineyards, In 1975 the winery was sold, and it changed hands more than once before it was purchased by Franciscan Estate in 1985. It became part of Constellation after Franciscan was sold. I remember the intensity of the Cabernet Sauvignon from the late seventies. Under Franciscan, production moved away from the focus on Cabernet Sauvignon and Chardonnay towards Bordeaux blends. Today the winery produces Napa Valley Cabernet Sauvignon, Rosenquist, and Elevation 1550 (a blend from the best lots in all three vineyards). The Reserve Red Blend is 88% Cabernet Sauvignon, 10% Malbec, and 2% Petit Verdot .

Outpost Wines

2075 Summit Lake Drive, Angwin, CA 94508
+1 707 965 1718
AXA Millesimes
info@outpostwines.com
www.outpostwines.com
Howell Mountain AVA

20 acres; 36,000 bottles
[map p. 36]

Outpost is high on Howell Mountain, more or less at the top of Summit Lake Drive, at 2,100 ft elevation. It was established in 1998 by Frank and Kathy Dotzler (are also partners in Mending Wall Winery, founded in 2014 together with winemaker Thomas Brown and others.) Outpost is unusual for Napa, because the flagship variety is Zinfandel (although this has become something of a specialty around Angwin). There is, of course, a varietal Cabernet Sauvignon, but also Petite Syrah and Grenache. The style is to harvest as late as possible for maximum ripeness. Outpost was sold in 2018 to AXA Millésimes, who own several châteaux in Bordeaux, and other wineries; this is their first venture in Napa Valley. Thomas Brown stays on as winemaker.

Peju Winery

8466 St. Helena Highway,
Rutherford, CA 94573
+1 707 963 3600
Tony Peju
customercare@peju.com
www.peju.com
Rutherford AVA

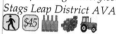

558 acres; 600,000 bottles
[map p. 36]

Tony and Herta Peju purchased 30 acres of vineyards in Rutherford in 1983: today Peju is a much larger operation, with the next generation of Lisa and Ariana now involved. A faux Castle, the winery is one of the more distinctive buildings in the area. Vineyards are in Rutherford, Pope Valley, and Calistoga, and there is a wide range of wines, including varietal Merlot, Cabernet Franc, Petit Verdot, Syrah, Zinfandel, Piccolo in reds, and Viognier, Riesling, Sauvignon Blanc in whites, as well as rosé and sparkling wine. The style is soft and crowd-pleasing, with an impression almost of sweetness. The tasting room is one of the few remaining that is always open. Peju bought the old Acacia winery in Carneros and turned into their second estate, Liana, in 2016.

Pine Ridge Winery

5901 Silverado Trail, Napa, CA
94558
+1 707 253 7500
concierge@pineridgewine.com
www.pineridgewinery.com
Stags Leap District AVA

309 acres; 1,000,000 bottles
[map p. 39]

Pine Ridge was one of the early wineries in Stags Leap, founded in 1978, focused on Cabernet Sauvignon from the area. In 2000, the founding family sold it to Crimson Wine Group, which is part of Leucadia National Corp. Today Pine Ridge also produces Cabernet Sauvignon cuvées from Rutherford, Oakville, and Howell Mountain, as well as Napa Valley bottling, and Chardonnay from Carneros. The style has moved from the restraint of the early years to more forward, soft, aromatic fruits. There is also an inexpensive blend of Chenin Blanc which comes from northern California (near Sacramento). There is a focus on oenotourism at the winery, which has one of the more popular tasting rooms in the area.

Plumpjack

620 Oakville Cross Road, Oakville,
CA 94562
+1 707 945 1220
John Conover
tastingroom@plumpjack.com
www.plumpjackwinery.com
Oakville AVA

42 acres; 120,000 bottles
[map p. 38]

Plumpjack is located on the site of the old Villa Mount Eden Winery (a famous Cabernet producer from the 1970s until it was bought out in 1986 by Stimson Lane. In 1994, Stimson Lane sold the site and moved production elsewhere). Plumpjack was started by Gavin Newsom and Gordon Getty and other investors in 1995. Grapes come from the vineyards surrounding the winery. The flagship wine is the Estate Cabernet Sauvignon. The style is forward and aromatic. The Merlot, Syrah, and Chardonnay come from other sites. Plumpjack has expanded into a portfolio of wineries, purchasing a 54 acre estate on Howell Mountain in 2005 to form CADE winery, which was expanded by purchasing another 82 acres in 2016. In 2012 they bought the 36 acre Stelzner vineyard in Stags Leap, which became Winery Odette.

Promontory

1601 Oakville Grade Rd, Oakville, CA 94562
+1 707 944 0125
concierge@promontory.wine
www.promontory.wine
Oakville AVA

79 acres; 25,000 bottles [map p. 38]

Famous for Harlan Estate (see profile), Bill Harlan started another project to produce wine at Promontory. He had first become interested in an 840 acre estate when he was looking for land for Harlan, but it did not become available to buy until twenty years after he had established Harlan Estate. Bill purchased the estate in 2008, and about 70% is being replanted, mostly with Cabernet Sauvignon. Located between Oakville and Yountville, it's about a mile south of Harlan Estate, with very steep terrain (15-40% slope), and diverse soil types, part sedimentary, part metamorphic, and a streak of volcanic terroir lower down. About 10% of the parcel was planted in the 1980s and 1990s (the grapes were sold). Straddling the border between AVAs, the vineyard has to have a Napa label, as it does not fall within either Oakville or Yountville. "It will fill in Napa's missing shade of red," Bill says. There are presently only about 30 acres in production, and the first release from the estate was the 2009 vintage. While Harlan Estate is known for being run in a reclusive style, Promontory is open for visits. It took several years of geological tests to decide on plantings. Built in an industrial style, the winery itself opened in 2017. The wine is a blend dominated by Cabernet Sauvignon, and smaller amounts of Malbec, Cabernet Franc, and Petit Verdot, and it ages partly in barriques of French oak, and partly in 30 hl barrels from Stockinger in Austria, with the proportion of Austrian oak increasing since they were introduced in 2012. Wines age in house for 5 years before release.

Quintessa

1601 Silverado Trail, Napa, CA 94559
+1 707 963 7112
Agustin Huneeus
info@quintessa.com
www.quintessa.com
Rutherford AVA

161 acres; 120,000 bottles [map p. 38]

Agustin Huneeus built Concha y Toro into a large producer in Chile, and was involved with estates in Napa Valley before he founded Huneeus Ventures in 1999. The portfolio includes several wineries, including Flowers in Sonoma and Benton Lane in Oregon, and is now run by his son Francisco. The 280 acre Quintessa property, located between the Silverado Trail and the Napa River in the Rutherford AVA, was purchased as virgin land in 1989, and planted with Bordeaux varieties: 129 acres of Cabernet Sauvignon, 26 acres of Merlot, 7 acres of Cabernet Franc, 4 acres of Petit Verdot, 4 acres of Carmenère, and just 2 acres of Sauvignon Blanc. Wine was made at Franciscan (in which Huneeus had a share) until the winery was completed in 2002. Quintessa is an unusual project in focusing on a single estate wine, with a varying blend of the Bordeaux varieties, aged in 8% new oak. A second wine, Faust, comes from a mixture of estate and purchased grapes. The Illumination cuvée of Sauvignon Blanc comes from the small plot at Quintessa together with purchased grapes from cooler climate vineyards, including some Sémillon; it ages in used barriques.

Quixote Winery

6126 Silverado Trail, Napa, CA 94558
+1 707 944 2659
B.R. Smith
info@quixotewinery.com
www.quixotewinery.com
Stags Leap District AVA

27 acres; 24,000 bottles [map p. 39]

The vineyard was originally part of Stags' Leap Winery (see mini-profile), but Carl Doumani kept it back when he sold Stags' Leap in 1997. The winery was designed by the eccentric Viennese artist Friedensreich Hundertwasser, whose basic principle was to avoid rectilinear features. The buildings look as though they come out of a fairy tale. Friedensreich also designed some of the funky labels. Carl focused on Petite Sirah, Cabernet Sauvignon, and Malbec, all produced as varietals. A rosé is made by saignée from Petite Sirah, partly with the intention of strengthening the red wine. The top wine is the Helmet of Mambrino Petite Sirah. Carl sold Quixote to Chinese company Jinta Vineyards in 2014.

Raymond Vineyard & Cellar

*849 Zinfandel Lane, St. Helena, CA
94574*

+1 800 525 2659

*customerservice@
raymondvineyards.com*

www.raymondwine.com

St. Helena AVA

*296 acres; 3,300,000 bottles
[map p. 37]*

Roy Raymond started as a cellar rat at Beringer the year after Prohibition. He married Martha Jane Beringer, and in 1971 they founded their own winery with the purchase of a 90 acre vineyard near St. Helena. Raymond sold the winery in 2009 to Jean-Charles Boisset of Burgundy, who already owned Deloach and Buena Vista in Sonoma. The winery has been renovated in Jean Charles's flamboyant style, and is well into oenotourism, with a variety of tasting packages offering quasi-theatrical experiences. Wines are divided into several ranges. The Estate Collection is the entry level, with Cabernet Sauvignon, Bordeaux blend, Chardonnay, and Sauvignon Blanc. The Small Lot Collection mostly focuses on other varietals. Generations is a step up with Napa Valley cuvées of Cabernet Sauvignon or Chardonnay. Distinct Collection includes Cabernet Sauvignons from almost all the individual AVAs.

Realm Cellars

*5795 Silverado Trail, Napa, CA
94558*

+1 707 224 1910

Benoit Touquette

team@realmcellars.com

www.realmcellars.com

Yountville AVA

20 acres; 72,000 bottles [map p. 38]

Realm started on the negociant model, owning no vineyards, but sourcing grapes from growers all over Napa Valley. The project started in 2002, when owner Juan Mercado made a switch from hospital administration to wine. The first wine came from To Kalon. There was a disaster with the 2003 vintage when the entire production was lost in a warehouse fire. Since the 2004 vintage, they have had a range of reds on the market, including Bard (a Bordeaux blend with about 70% Cabernet Sauvignon that is the largest production at about 500 cases), and the single vineyard cuvées, Farella (100% Cabernet Sauvignon from a (relatively) cool vineyard in Coombsville), and Dr. Crane (97% Cabernet Sauvignon and 3% Petit Verdot). Tempest is a blend dominated by Merlot, with Cabernet Sauvignon and Petit Verdot, while Falstaff is 60% Cabernet Franc with 40% Cabernet Sauvignon. White was introduced in 2010 with a Sauvignon Blanc from the Farella vineyard. The first estate vineyard was purchased in 2015 with a 20 acre block facing Stags Leap, which came together with a barebones winery (formerly the Hartwell estate). Moonracer is a Bordeaux blend with 75% Cabernet Sauvignon from the estate. Absurd is the top wine, a blend that can be completely different from year to year in both varieties and sources.; the 2005 (first) vintage was 38% Petit Verdot; the 2015 was 88% Cabernet Sauvignon, and it's intended to be the most hedonistic wine produced in the valley each year.

Frank Family Vineyards

*1091 Larkmead Ln, Calistoga, CA
94515*

+1 707 942 0859

Rich Frank

info@frankfamilyvineyards.com

www.frankfamilyvineyards.com

Calistoga AVA

*380 acres; 1,200,000 bottles
[map p. 36]*

The winery is located on a property that includes the historical Larkmead Winery (no connection with the present Larkmead label), a stone building constructed in 1884, and one of the oldest in Napa. The present winery was founded in 1992 by former Disney Studios President, Rich Frank. The tasting rooms are filled with film memorabilia. The specialty here is sparkling wine and Chardonnay, but the wide range extends beyond Cabernet Sauvignon to Zinfandel and Pinot Noir and less common varieties such as Sangiovese and Petite Sirah. The top wines both come from Rutherford: Patriarch is 100% Cabernet Sauvignon, and Winston Hill is a

Bordeaux blend with 91% Cabernet Sauvignon, and age for 21 months with 75% new oak: they are available only at the winery. Visitors often feel that the cost of the tasting for a flight of 4 wines is on the high side for Napa.

Robert Biale Vineyards

4038 Big Ranch Road Napa, CA 94558
+1 707 257 7555
Tres Goetting
customerservice@biale.com
www.biale.com
Oak Knoll AVA

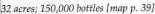

32 acres; 150,000 bottles [map p. 39]

Robert Biale is unusual in Napa for focusing on Zinfandel: in fact, there is not even a single cuvée of Cabernet Sauvignon. The history of the Biale family was tied up with growing Zinfandel, and Robert started the winery with some partners in 1991. Today the winery produces 14 cuvées of Zinfandel, mostly from single vineyards. Estate grapes come from the small (8 acre) vineyard around the vineyard in Oak's Knoll and Aldo's vineyard, just south of the winery on the outskirts of Napa, which still has the original bush vines from 1937. Purchased grapes come from several vineyards in Sonoma. Biale also produces 5 cuvées of Petite Syrah.

Robert Craig Wine Cellars

625 Imperial Way, Napa, CA 94558 (tasting room)
2475 Summit Lake Drive, Angwin, CA 94508 (winery)
+1 707 252 2250
Rachel Miller
info@robertcraigwine.com
www.robertcraigwine.com
Howell Mountain AVA

35 acres; 100,000 bottles [map p. 36]

Robert Craig was always interested in mountain vineyards. He founded his own estate in 1992, and the first release was from Mount Veeder. The winery, well up Howell Mountain at an elevation of 2,300 ft, was completed in 2002. Robert retired in 2012, and his longtime partner Elton Slone now runs the winery. There are separate cuvées of Cabernet Sauvignon from Mount Veeder and Spring Mountain as well as Howell Mountain, as well as the Affinity cuvée, which comes from Mount George just south of Stag's Leap. They are generally about 90% Cabernet Sauvignon, with the rest coming from Cabernet Franc, Merlot, Malbec, or Petit Verdot. They are typical mountain wines, with dense black fruits and strong tannic support. There are also varietal Merlot and Zinfandel, and the latest cuvée is Côte de Craig, a Grenache-Syrah blend from Howell Mountain. All are single-vineyard wines, with 80% of the grapes coming from the estate. The winery is not the most accessible, but there is a tasting room in downtown Napa.

Robert Keenan Winery

3660 Spring Mtn Rd, St. Helena, CA 94574
+1 707 963 9177
Michael Keenan
info@keenanwinery.com
www.keenanwinery.com
St. Helena AVA

49 acres; 156,000 bottles [map p. 36]

The property was actually one of the very first mountain wineries, functioning until Prohibition, and was then abandoned until retired insurance broker Robert Keenan bought it in 1974. His son Michael has been in charge since 1995. The estate is located down a long track off Spring Mountain Road, most of the way to Sonoma. The winery was renovated in 2015. Plantings are mostly Cabernet Sauvignon, Merlot, and Chardonnay, but there are also cuvées of Syrah, Zinfandel, and Cabernet Franc. Michael introduced a Cabernet -Merlot blend in 2011. The Napa Valley cuvées are blends of estate grapes with grapes sourced from other regions—Pope Valley for the Cabernet Sauvignon, Carneros for the Merlot. Spring Mountain cuvées come solely from the estate. Wines age in a mix of French and American oak, with 33% new wood for the Cabernet Sauvignon.

Rombauer Vineyards

3522 Silverado Trail, St. Helena, CA 94574
+1 800 622 2206
Koerner Rombauer
info@rombauer.com
www.rombauervineyards.com
St. Helena AVA

699 acres; 600,000 bottles
[map p. 36]

Koerner and Joan Rombauer were involved with several wineries in Napa Valley, starting as partners in Conn Creek, then founding their own estate in 1980 with a 7 ha vineyard of Zinfandel. The estate is now in the hands of the third generation. Built in 1982, the winery was also a custom crush facility. There's a strong focus on Chardonnay and Zinfandel (although it's mostly not sourced from Napa) as well as Cabernet Sauvignon. The Carneros Chardonnay comes from estate vineyards plus other growers, and there are also two single vineyard cuvées. The Proprietor Selection is the top Chardonnay, and is made only in top vintages—typically every 3-4 years—by barrel selection of the best lots. Winemaking is classic: whole cluster pressing, barrel fermentation, battonage every two weeks, all intended for a richness of style. Similar principles are followed for the Zinfandel: there's a basic cuvée blended from various regions, a Napa Valley cuvée, single vineyard cuvées (from the Sierra Foothills and Amador County), and the Proprietor Selection in top vintages. The style is classic California. Cabernet Sauvignon cuvées come from Napa Valley, with several single vineyard cuvées as well as the Diamond Selection, which is a blend of the best lots from several sites. Le Meilleur du Chai is a Bordeaux blend selected from the best lots. In addition to the Napa winery, there is also now a tasting room in the Sierra Foothills, where Rombauer purchased the Renwood Winery in 2019.

V. Sattui Winery

1111 White Lane, St. Helena, CA 94574
+1 707 963 7774
Dario Sattui
info@vsattui.com
www.vsattui.com
St. Helena AVA

630 acres; 600,000 bottles

This is really a double-take. In the nineteenth century, Vittorio Sattui started as a baker, made some wine at home, and then moved into commercial production. The winery closed in 1920 because of Prohibition. In 1976, Vittorio's great grandson, Dario, started with a delicatessen and a small winery, named after Vittorio; in 1984 he built a larger winery. He also subsequently founded the Castello di Amorosa winery in Napa. The range of Sattui wines is unusually broad, with more than 60 different releases, ranging from Sonoma and Napa to Amador Count, and including red, white, rosé, sparkling, and sweet wines. The top line is the Reserve Stock, with Chardonnay, Pinot Noir, Merlot, and Cabernet Sauvignon, all labeled as Napa Valley AVA. Estate vineyards account for 70% of production.

Scarecrow Wine

5055 Solano Avenue, Napa, CA 94558
+1 707 963 3361
info@scarecrowwine.com
www.scarecrowwine.com
Rutherford AVA

[map p. 38]

Scarecrow Wine is synonymous with the J.J. Cohn Estate. J.J. Cohn was Chief of Production at MGM Studios (where he made the Wizard of Oz). He was persuaded in 1945 by his neighbor John Daniel at Inglenook, to plant 80 acres of Cabernet Sauvignon on his property in Rutherford, which he had bought for a summer home. John Daniel bought all the grapes for Inglenook. The property has some old vines, because it bucked the trend to replant on AxR1 in the 1960s and stayed on St. George rootstock, on which there are still vines dating from 1945. J.J. Cohn's grandson Bret Lopez and his wife

Mimi DeBlasio own the estate today. Grapes were all sold until Scarecrow (named for the Wizard of Oz) was produced in 2003. It is 100% Cabernet Sauvignon from 2 acres of the vines planted in 1945, dry farmed, fermented for about three weeks, and then aged in French barriques with mostly new oak. M. Étain is a second wine from a block in the lower part of the Scarecrow vineyard. It is a blend of around 82% Cabernet Sauvignon, 9% Petit Verdot, 6% Malbec, and 3% Merlot, in a more fruit-forward style than Scarecrow. M. Étain is offered to the entire mailing list each year, but Scarecrow is a cult wine that is more difficult to obtain.

Seavey Vineyard

1310 Conn Valley Road, St. Helena, CA 94574

+1 707 963 8339

Jessica Rose

wine@seaveyvineyard.com

www.seaveyvineyard.com

St. Helena AVA

[!] [$60] [icons]

40 acres; 42,000 bottles

[map p. 36]

Formerly a wine-producing estate—known for its "claret"— the property became a horse and cattle ranch after Prohibition. William and Mary Seavey purchased the estate in 1979 and started growing grapes, which they sold to Raymond Vineyards. Wine production started in 1990 in a renovated stone barn in the center of the vineyards. The Seavey's daughter Dorie took over in 2016. Production is mostly red, based on varietal Cabernet Sauvignon and Merlot. The entry level Cabernet is the Caravina cuvée, a blend of 86% Cabernet Sauvignon with 11% Petit Verdot and 3% Merlot, aged in 40% new French oak. The Cabernet Sauvignon with no further name is a 100% varietal, aged in 60% new French oak. Founders' Reserve is the top wine, a barrel selection that's a blend of 99% Cabernet Sauvignon with 1% Merlot, aged in 100% new oak. The Merlot is 99% Merlot with 1% Cabernet Sauvignon, aged in 25% new oak. The only white is a Chardonnay. Caravina Cabernet is about half of production; all the other wines are produced in very small amounts. Philippe Melka is the consulting winemaker. Seavey is known for holding back a quarter of each vintage, so that older wines are available.

Silver Oak Cellars

915 Oakville Crossroad, Oakville, CA 94562 (Napa Winery)

7300 Hwy 128, Healdsburg CA 95458 (Alexander Valley winery)

+1 800 273 88097079427026

customercare@silveroak.com

www.silveroak.com

Oakville AVA

[walk] [$10] [icons]

400 acres; 1,200,000 bottles

[map p. 36]

Silver Oak started as a collaboration between entrepreneur Ray Duncan and winemaker Justin Meyer to produce Cabernet Sauvignon in an approachable style. The first estate vineyards were located in Alexander Valley and were the basis for the wine from the first vintage in 1972. The cellars in Napa Valley were built on the site of an old dairy farm, but the Napa vineyards did not come on line until 1979. The Alexander Valley cuvée is 100% Cabernet Sauvignon; the Napa Valley cuvée, which comes from a mix of estate and purchased grapes, is a Bordeaux blend based on Cabernet Sauvignon. The wines are aged in American oak, which explains their strong impression of vanillin and coconut; indeed, at one time the winery was known as Slather Oak in the trade. Justin Meyer sold back his share in the company to Ray Duncan in 2001. A second winery was built in Geyserville, and was replaced by a new winery close to Healdsburg in 2018. The company is run today by Ray's sons, David and Tim. They also own Twomey Cellars, producing Pinot Noir and Sauvignon Blanc, from wineries in Calistoga and Healdsburg. In 2017, Silver Oak purchased the Ovid winery and its 15 acres of vineyards on Pritchard Hill.

Silverado Vineyards

6121 Silverado Trail, Napa, CA 94558
+1 707 257 1770
Jon Emmerich
retail@silveradovineyards.com
www.silveradovineyards.com
Napa Valley AVA

400 acres; 840,000 bottles [map p. 39]

Silverado Vineyards was founded when Ron Miller and his wife Diane Disney (Walt Disney's daughter) bought two parcels of land off the Silverado Trail which they combined in 1978. The property included vineyards, and wine production started in 1981. The home estate vineyard of 170 acres in the Stags Leap district is now only part of the holdings, which include Miller Ranch vineyard close by in Yountville, Soda Creek Vineyard on the other side of the Silverado Trail, Mt. George Vineyard in Coombsville, and Firetree and Vineburg vineyards in Carneros. The range of Cabernet Sauvignons expresses the vineyards in Napa. The Estate Cabernet Sauvignon is a blend from Stags Leap and Coombsville, SOLO comes from a Heritage Clone planted in the home vineyard in 1968, GEO comes from Mt. George, and the Limited is a barrel selection of the best lots each year. The only cuvée that does not come from estate vineyards is Oakville Station, from the University of California's experimental plot in Oakville. There are two cuvées of Merlot, from Stags Leap and Mt. George, and also Cabernet Franc, Merlot, and Sangiovese varietals. In whites, there's a Chardonnay and a Sauvignon Blanc. Silverado Vineyards is unusual in maintaining an extensive collection of older vintages, with some cuvées available from as far back as 1990.

Sinegal Estate Winery

2125 Inglewood Avenue, St. Helena, California
+1 707 244 1187
David Sinegal
info@sinegalestate.com
www.sinegalestate.com
St. Helena AVA

10 acres; 80,000 bottles [map p. 37]

Starting from the nineteenth century when vines were planted here (it was then called the Inglewood Estate), the property has gone in and out of wine production. After many changes of ownership, it was purchased in 2013 by David Sinegal, son of the cofounder of giant Costco. After buying the 30 acre estate for $17 million, he spent another $8 million on renovations. The winery was renovated, new caves were excavated, and tasting room was built. The winery is state of the art, with many small tanks allowing plot-by-plot vinification. Vineyards range from valley floor to the slopes at the start of the Mayacamas Mountains. The two major wines are the Cabernet Sauvignon and Reserve Cabernet Sauvignon, both about 85% Cabernet Sauvignon, with Malbec, Petit Verdot, and Merlot as the other varieties. The Cabernet ferments in vat (85% stainless steel and 15% oak), and ages in 85% new oak while the Reserve ferments in a mix of vats and barriques, and ages entirely in new oak. The Cabernet Franc comes from plots including old vines, and ages in new oak. The Sauvignon Blanc (which has 40% of the Sauvignon Musqué clone) follows the style of Fumé Blanc, aged in barriques with a third new oak. The Cabernets and Sauvignon are Napa Valley AVA. There is also a Pinot Noir from Sonoma Coast.

St. Supéry Wines

8440 St. Helena Highway, Rutherford, CA 94573
+1 707 963 4507
wineclub@stsupery.com
www.stsupery.com
Rutherford AVA

556 acres; 420,000 bottles [map p. 36]

The Skalli family started making wine in Algeria, expanded into Corsica, and in 1982 bought the Dollarhide estate of over 1,500 acres, much of it used for cattle ranching, but including 500 acres of vineyards. Another 56 acres in Rutherford were bought in 1985, and the St. Supéry winery was constructed there in 1989. There are two lines of wines: Bordeaux varietals from the Rutherford estate; and a wider range from Dollarhide, including Chardonnay, Sauvignon Blanc, and Sémillon. I have usually found the wines to be somewhat simple. The Wertheimer brothers of Chanel, who own Châteaux Rauzan-Ségla in Margaux and Canon in St. Emilion, bought St. Supéry in 2015. It will be interesting to see if the style changes.

Stags' Leap Winery

6150 Silverado Trail, Napa, CA
94558
+1 707 944 1303
Christophe Paubert
stagsleap@stagsleap.com
www.stagsleapwinery.com
Stags Leap District AVA

84 acres; 960,000 bottles [map p. 39]

The apostrophe is the crucial identifier of this winery. Stag's Leap Winery is an old property, dating from 1893. Carl Doumani re-established the estate in 1972. The better known Stag's Leap Wine Cellars (see profile) was founded by Warren Winiarski in 1970. After a lawsuit about the right to use Stags Leap (the AVA has no apostrophe), both wineries were allowed to use the name, but with different usage of apostrophes. The focus, as always in Stags Leap, was on Cabernet Sauvignon. The Napa cuvée today is 86% Cabernet Sauvignon (with 6% Malbec, 4% Merlot, 2% Petite Sirah, and 2% Petit Verdot), and includes sources from other areas as well as Stags Leap. It ages in about one third new oak. The Audentia cuvée, introduced in 2010, is an unusual blend of 76% Cabernet Sauvignon with 18% Petite Sirah, 4% Malbec, and 2% Petit Verdot, aged in 50% new French oak. The Leap Cabernet Sauvignon is a blend of the best lots from older plots in the estate vineyard, aged in 50% new barriques. Carl Doumani was fond of Petite Sirah, so that has always been a feature of production, and after he sold Stag's Leap to Beringer in 1997, he kept a small vineyard back to make Petite Sirah; this became the Quixote Winery (see mini-profile), which Carl ran until he sold it to a Chinese firm in 2014.

Sterling Vineyards

1111 Dunaweal Lane, Calistoga,
CA 94515
+1 707 942 3344
svconcierge@svclub.com
www.sterlingvineyards.com
Calistoga AVA

1200 acres; 4,800,000 bottles
[map p. 36]

The most spectacular feature about Sterling is the approach, which makes it a major tourist site. The winery is located 300 ft above Calistoga, and access is by a small cable car. On my first visit, the system stuck; the emergency escape is to knock out a panel in the floor and descend by rope ladder to the forest below. Fortunately, after swinging in the wind for half an hour, the system restarted. The winery remains as striking as ever, but the wines unfortunately have lost their pizzazz. The winery was founded by Peter Newton in 1964, and released its first vintage in 1969: it was sold to Coca-Cola in 1977. (Peter Newton then started Newton Vineyard, which he later sold to LVMG.) Sterling was later sold to Seagram, became part of Diageo, and then was among the wineries sold to Treasury Wine Estates in 2015. In its heyday, Sterling was well regarded for its estate Cabernet and Chardonnay, which were among the wines that made the running in Napa in the early 1970s. Subsequent corporate takeovers turned it into a brand.

Stewart Cellars

6752 Washington St, Yountville,
CA 94599
+1 707 963 9160
James Stewart
info@stewartcellars.com
www.stewartcellars.com
Yountville AVA

0 acres; 60,000 bottles
[map p. 39]

After Michael Stewart sold Texas Microsystems in 2002, he moved into producing wine. Previously he owned Juliana Vineyard in Pope Valley, later sold to Terlato, and in 2000 he started Stewart Cellars, based on a negociant model of purchasing grapes. His son James is the general manager, and his daughter Caroline, together with her husband Blair Guthrie, are the winemakers. Paul Hobbs is the consultant winemaker. There are three ranges. Under the Stewart Cellars label, Cabernet Sauvignon and Sauvignon Blanc come from Napa Valley, while Chardonnay and Pinot Noir come from Sonoma. Long term contracts ensure consistency of sources. There is a second label called Slingshot for wines at a lower price point. The top range is called Nomad, sourced from six Beckstoffer vineyards (To Kalon, Bourn, Las Piedras, Georges III, Dr. Crane, and Missouri Hoppe), available only by mailing list.

Stony Hill Vineyard

3331 Saint Helena Highway North,
St Helena, CA 94574
+1 707 963 2636
Chris Hall
info@stonyhillvineyard.com
www.stonyhillvineyard.com
St. Helena AVA

40 acres; 60,000 bottles
[map p. 36]

Stony Hill is an icon in Napa Valley for its early production of Chardonnay. Fred and Eleanor McCrea purchased the property in 1943 and planted their first Chardonnay in 1947. The first vintage of the Chardonnay, produced in a lean style without malolactic fermentation, was 1952. Staying with white grapes, subsequently they planted Riesling and Gewürztraminer. The vineyards are all dry farmed. Alcohol levels are moderate for Napa Valley. The Chardonnay is the Wente clone; it's fermented in a mix of stainless steel and old oak, and ages in old barriques. Even today, after a half century of changes in fashion, it remains one of Napa Valley's best-known Chardonnays. Fred and Eleanor's son Peter took over in 1991, his daughter Sarah joined in 2011, and the wines continued to be made by winemaker Mike Chelini. The Chardonnay has a restrained style, showing floral notes with a touch of citrus. Cabernet Sauvignon was planted in 2004, and this too shows a relatively light, restrained style. In 2018, a majority share in Stony Hill was sold to Long Meadow Ranch (see mini-profile), a somewhat larger, but also family-owned, winery. The plan is to improve distribution but to leave the wines unchanged.

To Kalon Vineyard Company

Oakville, CA 94562
+1 833 401 0743
Andy Erickson
info@tokalonvineyardcompany.com
www.tokalonvineyardcompany.com
Oakville AVA

6,000 bottles

To-Kalon is a famous, perhaps the most famous, name in Napa Valley. Much of the vineyard is owned by Robert Mondavi, which in turn is owned by Constellation Brands, and Andy Beckstoffer owns a part that has is used to produce several high-profile single-vineyard wines. In 2019, Constellation announced the establishment of To Kalon Vineyard Company to produce wines from the vineyard, with famed winemaker Andy Erickson in charge. Andy makes wines for many producers as well as running his own winery, Favia (see mini-profile). The first release is the 2016 vintage of a 100% Cabernet Sauvignon from To Kalon, called Highest Beauty. It remains to be seen what other cuvées will follow, and whether this will impact the character of Robert Mondavi's To Kalon Cabernet Sauvignon. Using the name To Kalon has been embroiled in controversy; Robert Mondavi trademarked the use of To Kalon; after lawsuits, Beckstoffer was allowed to use it for cuvées from his plots.

Tor Kenward Family Wines

Wheeler Farms, Zinfandel Lane, St.
Helena, CA 94574
+1 707 963 3100
Tor Kenward
info@torwines.com
www.torwines.com
St. Helena AVA

0 acres; 40,000 bottles
[map p. 37]

Tor Kenward was an executive at Beringer before he retired and founded his own winery in 2001 to focus on small production runs of single vineyard Cabernet Sauvignon and Chardonnay. Grapes are purchased from top vineyards: production is less than 400 cases for each Cabernet cuvée and less than 100 cases for each Chardonnay. There are also cuvées of Syrah, Petite Syrah, and Grenache. Although there are no conventional winery visits at such, it's possible to make an appointment to visit at Wheeler Farms (a rather up-market custom crush facility) or to taste the wines at Maisonry in Yountville.

Turley Wine Cellars

3358 St. Helena Highway, St.
Helena, CA 94574
+1 707 963 0940
Helen Turley
tasting@turleywinecellars.com
www.turleywinecellars.com
St. Helena AVA

74 acres; 300,000 bottles [map p. 37]

Larry Turley was a co-founder of Frog's Leap Winery (see mini-profile) but left to form an independent venture in 1993. The original winery is in St. Helena; a second winery was established later in Templeton in San Luis Obispo to the south). Wines can be tasted in Templeton but not in Napa. The focus is on Zinfandel, with 26 cuvées (most come from Central Coast, with a handful from farther north) and Petite Syrah (cuvées) out of a total of 47 wines coming from 50 different vineyards. Larry's sister is Helen Turley, another well known winemaker.

Venge Vineyards

4708 Silverado Trail , Calistoga, CA
94515
+1 707 942 9100
Kirk Venge
info@vengevineyards.com
www.vengevineyards.com
Calistoga AVA

27 acres; 48,000 bottles
[map p. 36]

The Venge family imported wine until Nils Venge became a winemaker, starting at Villa Mount Eden and then Groth, where he established a reputation for making Cabernet Sauvignon. He purchased Saddleback Cellars (see mini-profile) in 1978 and made his first vintage there in 1982. In 1992 they changed the name formally to Venge Vineyards, although Saddleback continues to operate under its original name. Nils's son Kirk took over in 2003, and expanded by purchasing a vineyard to the east of the Silverado Trail just south of Calistoga which now functions under the official name of Venge Vineyards. Kirk makes wines under the names of both estates. Under Venge Vineyards, the Silencieux Cabernet Sauvignon comes from the Calistoga estate, supplemented by grapes from other vineyards, Scout's Honor is a blend based on Zinfandel with Petite Sirah, Carbono, and Syrah, and the Spettro white is based on Chardonnay with Viognier and Vermentino. A series of single-vineyard wines includes a wide range of varieties—Cabernet Sauvignon, Merlot, Zinfandel, Pinot Noir, Sangiovese, Chardonnay, Sauvignon Blanc, and Vermentino. The top wines from the Oakville estate are labeled as Venge Vineyards. The Family Reserve Cabernet Sauvignon has a production of only around 300 cases, but the DLCV Cabernet Sauvignon is the peak, with only one or two barrels produced. Venge Vineyards expanded with the purchase in 2016 of Robert Rue Winery in Russian River Valley; renamed Croix Estate, Kirk produces Pinot Noir and Chardonnay there. Kirk is also well known as a flying winemaker, making wine at many properties in Napa Valley.

Vine Hill Ranch

7353 St, Helena Highway, Napa,
CA 94599
+1 707 944 8130
Bruce Philipps
vhr@vinehillranch.com
vinehillranch.com
Oakville AVA

69 acres; 10,000 bottles
[map p. 38]

This is an old property, but its move to the modern style is more recent. Bruce Kelham purchased the ranch of more than 400 acres in 1959 on the slopes of the Mayacamas mountains when it was used for polyculture: farming hay (at the bottom), growing walnuts, and growing various grape varieties (but not Cabernet). Bruce's daughter Alexandra and her husband Bob Phillips took over in 1978 and started the move to current varieties when they were forced to replant by phylloxera in 1985. Their children run the property today. Originally all the grapes were sold, but since 2008 the Phillips have made a Cabernet Sauvignon as a selection from seven blocks. An original feature is that the label lists all seven blocks, and those used in any particular year are punched out on the label. The wine shows typical Oakville power and elegance.

Volker Eisele Family Estate

3080 Lower Chiles Valley Rd, St. Helena, CA 94574-9632
+1 707 965 2260
Alexander & Catherine Eisele
info@volkereiselefamilyestate.com
volkereiselefamilyestate.com
St. Helena AVA

59 acres; 48,000 bottles
[map p. 36]

Volker and Liesel Eisele bought the property in Chiles Valley in 1974, and grew grapes and made wine on a semi-professional basis until they started commercial production in 1991. Their son Alexander runs the estate today. The wines are made at the Napa Wine Co custom crush facility in Oakville, and can be tasted at the tasting room there. The focus is on Bordeaux blends. The best known wines are Terzetto (an equal blend of Cabernet Sauvignon, Cabernet Franc, and Merlot), the Estate Cabernet Sauvignon a (blend of 78% Cabernet Sauvignon with Merlot). and the Sievers Reserve Cabernet Sauvignon (single-vineyard wine from a 7 acre plot). The white Gemini is a 3:1 blend of Sémillon with Sauvignon Blanc.

von Strasser Winery

965 Silverado Trail, Calistoga, CA 94515
+1 707 942 9500
Rudy von Strasser
info@vonstrasser.com
www.vonstrasser.com
Calistoga AVA

0 acres; 12,000 bottles
[map p. 36]

This winery has had two incarnations. Rudy and Rita von Strasser established a winery on Diamond Mountain in 1990, where they specialized in cuvées based on Cabernet Sauvignon, mostly from the 35 acre estate. They sold the estate in 2015, but retained the rights to the von Strasser brand, which they restarted by buying the Lava Vine winery in Calistoga in 2016. Lava Vine produced a series of cuvées from unusual grapes from a variety of appellations outside Napa, and these have been retained under the same name. Under the von Strasser label there is now a series of seven cuvées based on Cabernet Sauvignon, with a general cuvée, five single-vineyard wines, and a Bordeaux blend called the Reserve, all from vineyards on Diamond Mountain which Rudy either owns or rents.

Whitehall Lane

1563 St. Helena Highway, St. Helena, CA 94574
+1 707 963 9454
Katie Leonardini
greatwine@whitehalllane.com
www.whitehalllane.com
St. Helena AVA

126 acres; 480,000 bottles
[map p. 37]

The site has been growing grapes for a long time, but the existing winery was founded in 1979 by the Finkelstein family, who sold it to the Leonardini family in 1993. In addition to the 25 acre estate vineyard around the winery, there are six vineyards in St. Helena, Rutherford, Yountville, and Oak Knoll, as well as one in Sonoma. There are Napa Valley varietal cuvées of Cabernet Sauvignon, Merlot, and Malbec, single-vineyard wines from the Leonardini and Millennium MM vineyards in Rutherford, and the Oak Glen vineyard in Oak Knoll, a Zinfandel from Sonoma, and a single vineyard Pinot Noir from Carneros.

Index of Estates by Rating

Index of Organic and Biodynamic Estates

Index of Estates by Varietal Specialty

Index of Estates by Appellation

Louis Martini Winery
Madrigal Vineyards
Melka Estates
Merryvale Wines
Morlet Family Vineyards
Newton Vineyard
Pahlmeyer Winery
Philip Togni Vineyard
Pride Mountain Vineyards
Raymond Vineyard & Cellar
Robert Keenan Winery
Rombauer Vineyards
Seavey Vineyard
Spottswoode Estate
Stony Hill Vineyard
Tor Kenward Family Wines
Turley Wine Cellars
Vineyard 29

Volker Eisele Family Estate
Whitehall Lane
Stags Leap District
Cliff Lede Vineyards
Clos du Val Winery
Pine Ridge Winery
Shafer Vineyards
Robert Sinskey Vineyards
Stag's Leap Wine Cellars
Stags' Leap Winery
Yountville
Bell Wine Cellars
Domaine Chandon Winery
Dominus Estate
Gemstone Vineyard
The Kapcsándy Family Winery
Lagier Meredith Vineyard
Realm Cellars

Index of Estates by Name